Our Foothills III
Another Anthology
by the
Foothills Writers

Thomas Blanton
Stephen Downing
Michael (MJ) FitzGerald
Gretchen Griffith
Stefanie Hutcheson
Linda McLaughlin LaRose
Kathy Lyday
Carol Starr
Lucy Wilkes

ISBN: 9798529556528

Imprint: Independently published

Our Foothills III

Table of Contents

Life in the Foothills

Life in the Foothills
by
Thomas Blanton

People drive slow in the left lane
So you have to pass on the right.
That's life in the Foothills.

You feel depressed and sad
So you put your convertible's top down and find a curvy road.
That's life in the Foothills.

Local politicians break ground for fast food joints
So you wonder why we can't have decent restaurants here.
The mountain scenery is a short drive away
So you run up to Blowing Rock for dinner.
That's life in the Foothills.

The summers are not too hot, the winters not too cold
So you can be reasonably comfortable most of the time.
This is where Floridians come to retire
So you have the chance to make new friends.
That's life in the Foothills.

Big cities in one direction and peaceful mountains in the other
So you have access to whatever you need.
Welcome to life in the Foothills.

Windy City
by
Kathy Lyday

Instead of eating my usual oatmeal at home, I decided to have breakfast at the Windy City Grill. Since moving south from Hudson (in southern Caldwell County) to Viewmont (just north of Hickory), I noticed that there were several establishments with the name Windy City: Windy City Grill, Windy City Sundries, and Windy City Barber Shop. Was there some sort of wind phenomenon in Viewmont that was unique to this locale? Why did Viewmont have so many Windy City businesses?

Chicago is often called the Windy City. I always assumed that this was due to the breeze from nearby Lake Michigan. Several years ago, I spent a week in Chicago in late March; that wind was memorable. I can also attest to the fact that it is windy in Viewmont because my broad-brimmed hats often fly away in the breeze. While mulling this over, I was reminded of the chorus to Bob Dylan's song, *Blowin' in the Wind*.

Apparently, Viewmont used to be named the Windy City so I went to the local library to find out why. I located a series of books entitled *The Catawbans* by Gary Freeze. Windy City was mentioned a few times, and there was a phrase in one of the books indicating that the Windy City might have been named after a bragging neighbor, but there were no definite details. I left a note for the librarian in the Carolina Room asking for additional information and was told he would contact me on Monday.

In the meantime, I asked several long-time Hickory residents why Viewmont had been called the Windy City. I spoke with John, who works at a local newspaper, and mentioned Chicago is called the Windy City. He informed me that Chicago's nickname had nothing to do with the weather. Chicago became known as the Windy City because a New Yorker accused Chicago politicians of "windiness" after they bragged about beating New York for the 1893 World's Fair bid. Newspaper guys remember that stuff. John suspected the Viewmont name was due to the same thing.

Randy, who had grown up in Hickory, said that the Windy City referred to flapping jaws, i.e., there was a lot of conversation going on when the men of Viewmont congregated daily to pass the time. That sounded plausible to me and warranted further exploration.

John and Randy were gentle with their answers, but I got the distinct sensation that behind their polite smiles, they were thinking that it was fruitless to be pursuing this. It was pretty obvious to them already.

Hoping to find out more, I talked to some older women who lived in Hickory for many years. I learned that the Windy City Grill used to be called Homer's many years ago, and was at one time located where the ABC Store on Hwy. 127 now sits. Before that, it was right in front of Viewmont Elementary School. I even spoke with a lady who actually got engaged there while splitting a grilled pimento cheese sandwich with her boyfriend. While these conversations were enjoyable, no one actually had information about why Viewmont had been called Windy City.

I even joined a *Facebook* group called "The Good, the Bad and the Ugly of Hickory," and posted my question. I got various answers ranging from Viewmont being the highest point in Hickory to the recurring response about gossiping men. Someone even said that there had been a Hickory citizen named Windy who was a colorful character, and the area had been named after him. Maybe that was a reference to the phrase I had found earlier in *The Catawbans*? This was so confusing; I just wanted to see an official print source that *I* considered legitimate and offered a reasonable explanation! Did anyone really know for *sure*?

Monday, as promised, I received an email from the librarian in charge of the Carolina Room. He sent me an article which answered my question. A feature article in the *Hickory Daily Record* dated May 27, 1993, reported some information that had been obtained from the owners of the Windy City Barber Shop: "There was a general store in Windy City where the gentlemen of the community gathered each day and they were called 'windbags.'"

This is why Viewmont was called the Windy City! In print! The name of the area was changed to Viewmont after completion of Viewmont Elementary School, which was in Hickory's first suburb.

Surely city leaders did not want to associate innocent children with the tawdriness of a school called Windy City Elementary?

I truly wished the story had been juicier and less of a copycat version of Chicago's situation. But now I knew and could close the book. To be honest, I was a bit deflated that the quest had ended. It had been refreshing to talk about something other than COVID, Putin, and rising gasoline prices.

So, this is why I visited the Windy City Grill for breakfast. I thought it would be a better fit for me than Windy City Sundries or Windy City Barber Shop. I sat at the counter and ordered one of their famous sandwiches: sausage, egg, and cheese. When the waitress delivered it, I asked her if she knew why this area had been called the Windy City. Without a second of hesitation, she responded: "It's 'cuz all the wind that blows through here." She pointed to the drive-through window. "You should see how the wind almost knocks us down when we have that thing open."

My friend, it was totally worth the cholesterol gain to hear that news. As I walked out to my car, I found myself singing the chorus of that Bob Dylan song again.

Foundations in the Foothills
by
Stefanie Hutcheson

Living in Caldwell County, North Carolina gives me much inspiration in my writing endeavors. Whether it's the climate, the people, the beauty of my surroundings, or the traditions, there is always something and/or someone worth describing.

For instance, the climate. Since the northern end of Caldwell County borders Watauga County, the difference between Highway 321 in the mountains and the southerly section below Caldwell County--bordering Burke and Catawba Counties--can be day and night. The northern edge has more snow and icy roads while the southern end can be dry as a cob--as well as have a significant temperature difference!

The people are a myriad of cultures as well. When I first moved to Lenoir in 2000, I interviewed for two different high schools. One was touted as being racially diverse and the other? It was not. West Caldwell High School had more students who came from farming, textile, and blue-collar households while South Caldwell seemed to be more of the white-collar variety.

Let's discuss the natural aesthetics of Caldwell County. Most of the locals know of Wilson's Creek and have imbibed in its cool waters. Fishing and canoeing and floating are all activities that entice folks out during all seasons--yes, it's true! Maybe not swimming but any time of year you will see kayaks and folks in their waders all along the creek. The John's River area is a popular spot for fishing also.

There are many beautiful mountain scenes in Caldwell County. A drive up through the Buffalo and Samson areas will provide wondrous photo opportunities, as will venturing through the backroads and the Globe areas. The Yadkin River offers more water opportunities, as well as large tracts of farmland to enjoy. Caldwell County has a little bit of almost everything for nature lovers to explore.

What would an anthology be without listing the traditions of the area? Back in 2000, Lenoir was known for being the "Furniture Capital of the World." As politics and world events took place, many of these jobs were sent overseas. This left the town to fall back on making new

6

fame for itself. Arts started to flourish; wineries and breweries began to make a mark on the area. Food trucks became a norm rather than an occasional diversion from the regular eating establishments. Speaking of which, as the town began its regrowth, more national franchises found a home here. Also, several boutiques and bookstores decided to settle in.

As COVID wreaked havoc on the world, Caldwell County took another hit. Between mandates and closures, some businesses faltered. Folks who had invested their lives in their shops soon found that they weren't immune (pardon the pun) to life's bumps and twists in the road. However, thanks to the human spirit and compassion of many, something wondrous happened: curbside service!

In the effort to keep our county from floundering, folks rallied together to order products online and drive up to receive them! While it wasn't the same, in some ways, it was better. How? It helped families to do more things together. Sitting around the table for meals became a norm again rather than the exception. The pandemic forced us to slow down and take stock. As we once again spent time with loved ones, new relationships flourished and forged. COVID, in some ways, had a silver lining to the Pandora's Box of Devastation that it tried to use to separate mankind.

Festivals are being planned again. Churches are seeing growth and offering more service times to accommodate the needs of the folks. Winter came, but you know what else arrived? Spring. Hope. Perseverance. The human spirit wavered but stood its ground. Life in the Foothills of North Carolina, specifically in my home of Caldwell County, continues. Through God's grace, we are still here. May He continue to bless our land, our homes, and our eyes as we witness His glory always, always, being revealed.

Moving South
by
Carol Starr

When my husband, Elliott, and I retired, we moved from the Hudson Valley in New York. We ended up in another Hudson, in North Carolina!

We were leaving the lovely wood-sided house in the woods, two miles from town. The light in the living room from the skylights meant we always knew what the weather was like when we walked into that space. Our two dogs thrived in the fenced-in yard. Once a bear climbed onto the deck off the master bedroom. White lilacs grew wild at an old foundation nearby and I had planted some by the front steps. It was quiet, only one neighbor. As we packed up a rented U-Haul truck, I already began to miss this house I had designed…my architect's dream.

Unfortunately, we couldn't afford the taxes, so we sold the house, and determined to move to a warmer climate. On a trip to North Carolina, we found a small house in a fairly new development. It had some nearby woods and was seven miles in either direction to a town.

My sister's then-boyfriend, Joe, said that the Foothills, east of the Blue Ridge Mountains, were the place to be. He had lived in Hickory all his adult life and liked the place and the people.

Since I had a license to drive a box truck, I got to drive the big U-Haul. Elliott drove our Subaru with the two dogs in the back seat. I pulled our other car, a smaller Toyota, on a two-wheel dolly hitched to the back of the truck.

It was a fun trip south, but not without adventure. When we reached Virginia, there was a billboard advertising "Virginia ham: All you can eat." Now there was something we just had to try.

We got off the interstate and pulled into the restaurant. It was cafeteria style. There was a rather large woman behind the counter. She would ask, "What do you want?" as she waved a large scoop.

"Well, I'd like some of that Virginia ham." She plopped two slices on a plate.

"And what else?"

"How about some potatoes?"

A large scoop of mashed potatoes landed on the plate.

"And what else?"

"The corn looks good…"

She plopped a scoop of corn on the plate.

"And what else?"

"Some of those nice, fluffy biscuits…"

Two biscuits landed on the now overflowing plate.

"And what else?"

That was all we could imagine eating. Disappointed, we found the Virginia ham extremely salty and the consistency of shoe leather. But the biscuits were fluffy, the mashed potatoes were satisfyingly tasty and filling, and the corn was tender and sweet.

That night we pulled into a motel. I asked where I could park the truck with its trailer. The clerk directed me to the back of the complex. I drove back there and parked the truck. In the morning, I realized I couldn't get out of there without backing up. No way was I going to try that. Finally, one of the truckers took pity on this little old truck-driving lady. "There's a paved lane on the other side of the outdoor pool. You can sneak around that way."

Whew, it worked. After that, I was very careful to scope out the parking lots.

Then, we drove down Route 77, which has some daunting grades. I cautiously geared down to provide some braking by the engine. Boy! I loved driving that big ol' truck!

We stayed at a motel near the house while we finalized the sale, then hired two husky men to unload the furniture and boxes.

I found I did like the little house. So did the dogs after we had a fence installed in the backyard. Neighbors were friendly and so were people at the Senior Center in Lenoir. One southern lady told me her secret to making good biscuits. I play Bridge early Thursday mornings. Elliott also plays bridge occasionally with a Wednesday afternoon group. (He doesn't like to get up early.)

After these fifteen years, we have many friends and love the Foothills and the beautiful Blue Ridge Parkway. I'm glad we moved here.

A Lament
by
Gretchen Griffith

The country store is no more.
Convenience has replaced character.

Modern computers now zing out printed receipts longer than an old man's cane. Gone is the ka-ching from the cash register announcing a sale. A plastic charge card replaced under-the-counter ledgers. "Jot it down, Mac. Payday is Thursday," or "Here, ma'am, I've set this aside for you. No charge," knowing full well paydays arrive few and far between for some families whose debts would never be reconciled. That's the way of the old country store in the Foothills.

The liars' bench outside, once a pew in the Methodist Church down the lane, is now replaced with a silver icebox stuffed with mounds of frozen bags waiting to cool the beer on the lake on a scorching end to a long week's work. This now absent bench once welcomed tired workers after a long day in the furniture plant. It was where Yellow-Dog Democrats bided their time and shook their heads, but not their fists, at those upstart Lincoln-Lovers passing by. Fisticuffs, they knew, were for behind the store or for defending the cause at the voting precinct, not here in front of the youngsters.

Hound dogs once slept on the front stoop so deeply they didn't notice children jumping over them to enter. Adults took it in stride. Literally. The deep snore and occasional growl is now replaced with the floofy pedigree yapper inside a dog purse complete with fake service dog papers. The swoosh of automatic doors silenced the slamming of the old screen doors that became inconvenient once air conditioning arrived. Fly swatters too became a thing of the past.

There is no more free candy for wide-eyed tykes pointing out their choices while their mothers load the counter with the weekly goods. Gone too are boiled eggs marinating in pickled beet juice and displayed in a gallon jar, their red drippings falling off the chins of delighted customers. There are no more gallon jars filled with fat, juicy dill pickles soaking in salty brine, nor the poor man's lunch...pickle, nabs, and a can of vienna sausages.

Where are the potbellied stoves that warmed hands and hearts for generations, with the daddies showing their finesse over red and black checkerboards and the grandpas holding court encircled by all who stopped by on a cold winter day?

There's no more after-hours stockroom gathering of the neighbors, no twang of the banjo or strumming of the guitars or thump-a-thump of the washtub bass string. Picking and grinning has been replaced by the throb of an audio system's bass blaring in the parking lot, bothersome rather than inviting. Passing down lyrics from the ancients no longer happens with ease when a country store has shuttered its windows. Nor does bringing up a new generation steeped in bluegrass traditions passed from one to the next in the comfort of friends rather than the sterile classroom lessons of instructors.

Friday night football games over, the teens arrived late to the gatherings, cheerleaders shod in saddle oxfords, their pompoms rustling to the beat of the music, quarterbacks busting with pride, or humiliation, whichever the case may be. They found acceptance at the store, and a safe place to fall as they navigated this new-to-them rite of passage. Old folks smiled, remembering their turns, guiding the youth with a wisdom only they have.

Saturday nights found another group, this one gathering around the Philco radio crackling out Nashville's Grand Ole Opry. Rural electric lines connected to their homes lessened the need to congregate, yet the crowds kept coming to the store. After all was said and done, listening to music was a corporate experience.

So too was listening to Roosevelt's Fireside Chats during the Great Depression, or even further generations back, anticipating the announcement on Armistice Day, the war is over, and rushing to the belfries of their respective churches to ring out the news so those at home, hearing the far-off peal, would know.

As we salute with our money the yellow-signed stores dotting the Foothills landscape, we cannot forget the price we truly pay. I lament our loss.

Leaving for the Foothills
by
Michael (MJ) FitzGerald

It was a long bus ride, with or without the vigilance required for a bicycle. Three hours by car becomes seven hours courtesy of Greyhound. Wide awake at boarding, if you draw the quiet passengers lot, you will be snoozing before too many townships; if you draw the lot of the entertaining traveling troubadour passengers, though, you will be wide awake till you are evicted for the next bus. There is usually a bus change every three hours (probably for the fun of aggravating passengers).

The advantage of being awake, of course, is knowing the bike you loaded below in luggage, having cajoled the driver not to upcharge you, is still where you loaded it. If you have some Greyhound miles behind you, and you are awake, you tend to notice the loads and unloads at each stop, having heard a few stories. Should you fall asleep, lulled by the motion and the silence (sweet following the hustle and stress of catching the bus) you may be running a risk. Take it from a snorer who once exited a bus to discover his sweat sock treasury had disappeared.

On this particular Greyhound adventure, I got to load and unload my bicycle on three different buses--for what could have been a three-hour drive by automobile. It did give me second thoughts as I waited for the last bus at Winston-Salem depot. I do remember the late summer sun baking the pavement while I wondered if the third bus would have luggage space for my bike. Not to mention wondering if this whole enterprise was a mistake.

I was moving away from a separated but caring family locale to a town and county where I knew absolutely no one and had hardly known of its existence before undertaking this exodus by bus. Essentially, I was conveying my worldly goods in a suitcase, along with a sleeping bag and a bike. On a hunch this truck driving course made sense.

Yeah, I had second thoughts. I wasn't even sure, in my fifties, I wanted to drive a truck. I did know I wanted a change from my minimum wage opportunities without a skilled trade in an academic, professional degree town. A temporary, above-average, metal construction job had just given me a depreciating "nest egg," so now, with the beginning of a new course semester, was the time to make the change, if it was to be accomplished. Thus, the leaving for the Foothills.

At any rate, the Greyhound gods happened to be favorable this particular day and I eventually exited at Hickory's official discharge point in the late 1990s, a Christian health food store on the west side of town. I then switched modes to possibly the longest taxi fare I have incurred, excepting prom night limousines in the Big City.

Luggage does not travel well on a twenty-mile bicycle ride. So, where is the backstory here? My twenty-mile taxi (it cost me $30) brought me to the Foothills I had 'researched' in late August. The town was Lenoir and the truck driving course was offered at Caldwell County Community College and Technical Institute. I figured if, in my fifties, I was going to become a truck driver, I had better learn from the best, where drivers had been running moonshine for generations, long before we had NASCAR.

I had placed a deposit on an apartment within bicycling distance to campus and had registered for driver training on my initial visit a couple of weeks earlier. The cab driver would not take $25, even though he could see me wavering on throwing my suitcase on my safely arrived bike and pedaling the twenty miles. Definitely one of my better decisions to pay the $30. Ever seen a guy on a bicycle, with a suitcase, pedal 20 miles on Hwy 321? Neither have I. There's a reason.

Safely enrolled in the driver's program, I found our lead instructor always carried his gun in his lunch bag on the road (before the days of commonplace concealed permits). Twenty-four plus years worth of the road, and a whole lot of miles. Smooth as syrup, and thorough. Backed by a couple of primary assistant instructors (both drivers for over 20 years, Over the Road--OTR--and regional) our primary instructor had at least one truck disappear on him and one taken at gunpoint.

Of our assistant instructors, one was a 'Nam infantry vet who was not syrup. He liked convoys with his buddies, and he liked "running" his truck on the edge of what the law allows. When asked by a student driver one day why he didn't "avoid the draft," he shared his honest reflection, to the effect, "We were at war, and we needed men, and we needed a draft. I just figured I was an American at the right age and, if I was drafted, I would serve. It was just normal. It was expected, and I figured I would do my share." He entered the military before the war became a heated, divisive, national controversy, but you got the definite feeling it would not have mattered. At the time of the telling, he just shrugged his shoulders as though it was perfectly normal for every American to do his duty, whatever his (or her) fate.

Our other lead assistant instructor was a tall Marine vet with ten-to-twelve years of service who taught flying lessons when he was not getting new drivers up to speed. He tended to be a taciturn, disciplined man with a keen sense of observing student drivers' skills, or lack thereof. His silence would eventually be punctuated by such anecdotes as his standing on top of a tanker truck in a fuel shed, loading, in the middle of the night, along with another driver at the adjacent fuel point loading his truck, when an overhead lightbulb burst, showering sparks in the direction of both trucks. By way of emphasis, the instructor paused and concluded his story. "There was a moment of pause when we both just looked at each other, and said nothing, knowing we had a bond" (as drivers who very nearly shared the same fate).

Once I had passed the driver's course, and was being put through the paces of driving trucks across America, I kept returning to the Foothills. Enjoyment of the outdoors, new friends and acquaintances, along with Lenoir becoming my 'default' location while on the road, may have been the primary motivators in choosing Lenoir as my base to write "(the) great American novel(s)." Trucking gave me the diminishing "nest egg" to write it. On being "great," though, needs to be determined, since all five hundred and fifty-five pages of it have been gathering dust for many years. If the future holds publication and acceptance, the leaving for the Foothills may generate unforeseen returns from book signings and travel adventures, though, most assuredly, not by means of our historic Greyhounds.

The Foothills
by
Lucy Wilkes

Before moving to the Foothills we purchased a video of the area. Seeing the magnificent scenery and hearing the mountain music, our hearts were won over. My husband and I knew we could be happy here.

Moving in and of itself is traumatic any way you look at it. The decision to move from Florida, our home, and family, to a place where we only knew our real estate lady, our pastor and his family, and the librarian took much prayer and direction from God and His word.

Preston and I were able to purchase our first house in Happy Valley and moved into it on September 22, 1994. We were captivated by the charm of the foothills of the mountains with their changing views every day, and each time of the day. The people in this area were friendly, saying good morning, and willing to help in any way they could--even when asking for directions or giving help with the car that time it got stuck when we turned around off the road.

One thing we learned quickly here is when asking how far it is to any place, instructions were given in minutes to get there instead of miles. In Florida, distances are in miles not minutes because it is flatland. Here in the Foothills, three miles might take thirty minutes to get to where you're going--but the views are worth the ride.

In Happy Valley there is the Yadkin River. It seemed small to us until it flooded the valley, then it was bigger than the Catawba River. During this rainy time, we moved into our new place. From baptism by clay in slick yards, to our well pump being hit by lightning, to our basement catching on fire, with seventeen inches of snow on the ground, we knew we were now like other Tarheels. Here was our home. We were not born in North Carolina, but we got here as soon as we could.

Zack's Fork Trail
by
Steve Downing

Exercise will keep you young - maybe even delay aging? Nah, probably not. Your joints know how old (and possibly worn out) you are.

It was running for many years. Then jogging. Now it's walking (hiking) and biking. My knees, ankles, and hips like me better for the change.

Zack's Fork Trail, on the north side of Lenoir near the Aquatic Center, is a favorite hiking and biking spot. Up and down terrain with an occasional mountain biker encounter. (Watch for the bikes!) Mountain bikes are stealthy and able to sneak up on one unawares easily. Hiking Zack's Fork Trail is good practice for maintaining one's 'situational awareness' as hikers and bikers can travel in either direction on the path. No glory in being ambushed by a biker…

Dirt trails, because they are uneven, demand that one pay attention to the path. It is boring to walk with a constant stride and an unvarying pace. 'Step-up,' 'step-down,' and 'scoot sideways' make for a more satisfying walk in my humble opinion. Likewise, a woodland trail offers the chance to see wildlife: birds, squirrels, a deer or two, and sometimes even a snake.

I park at the ball fields. Cross the creek and walk around the soccer field to start the trail. The first half (no matter whether you go clockwise or counterclockwise) is predominantly uphill. Downhill from the halfway point. Level finish back to parking.

Good to get out in nature for a time. I wish I didn't have to drive in order to 'walk,' but the neighborhood dogs still don't recognize me or my wife - after nearly thirty years in the same 'hood.

Meanwhile, Zack's Fork Trail remains my sylvan choice for exercise.

The Great Outdoors

Poplar Leaves
by
Stephen Downing

The trees between my house and the neighbors' pond are pretty much leafless now. The leaves have turned from green to reds and yellows and browns, and leapt from their branches to the ground. Normally I would rake or leaf blower them into piles, but not this year. They can just lay where they've fallen. Hurts my back to rake much anymore. Besides, 'Yard of the Month' winner has never been on my bucket list...

I have one large, tall poplar tree that is visible out of our second bathroom's window. It is completely bare now except for two green leaves residing on a single branch. They are the only leaves on the tree and they are still green. One, like a sweater on a hanger in my closet, shimmies and twists in the wind. The other, with a sky-reaching vertical stem, soars like a kite on a string. They seem to be tenacious in refusing to acknowledge that fall is over and winter is coming.

I know it's silly, but I told my wife that I had named them Peter and Paul. I imagine that they are siblings who have sworn a pact to hang onto their shared branch until Christmas Eve. They are determined to see Santa fly overhead. Thanksgiving has passed and I am rooting for them. If one or both should depart from their lofty perch, I will find them where they land. I've promised to place them in our house next to the cookies and cocoa so that they can meet Santa on Christmas Eve.

Dateline December 1st: very windy. Sometime during the night, Peter left his tree branch and plummeted to the ground. Paul looked so forlorn all by himself that morning when I looked out the window. After breakfast I went into the yard to look for Peter. I couldn't find him. I apologized to Paul.

Later that day I took one last look for Peter. I found him! Lying face down in the creek in the backyard, I knew it was Peter right away. He was green with a touch of brown on his stem. I pulled him out of the water and placed him on the garage workbench to dry. I will yet introduce him to Santa! And Paul too, if he also decides to drop.

Dateline December 5th: Paul left the limb during the night. I looked out the window at a barren branch. I could see Paul on the ground almost directly underneath. I went out and retrieved him. He now rests alongside Peter in the garage. Next adventure for the pair is Christmas Eve and, hopefully, a meet-up with Santa.

Doggone Dogwoods
by
Lucy Wilkes

"Alexa, what kind of dogwood trees grow in North Carolina?" I asked.

That's when the internet went down. *What will I do now?* So I asked Google. Oh yeah, no internet. Next, I went and got the encyclopedia to find out what I needed to know. Books are always ready with the answers to be found.

This is what I came across. There are three species of dogwood trees that exist in North Carolina.

One of the most common dogwood trees is the alternate-leaf dogwood. It grows in the mountains, but not in the northern mountains. The leaves and white flowers share alternating space on the branches. These dogwood trees can reach up to thirty-five feet with a canopy of white flowers across the top of the tree resembling a crown.

Also, a bush-like gray dogwood tree grows in the meadows of the mountains of the northwestern corner of North Carolina. It has gray-to-white berries and gray twigs that the wildlife enjoys eating seasonally.

The flowering dogwood is common in the wild and is popular as an ornamental tree. People are enchanted every spring as the flowers burst forth amidst a majestic tapestry of colors of white, pink, and dark pink across the mountains.

I discovered that in 1941, North Carolina chose the dogwood flower as its state flower. Interesting facts are found in books when they can't be located in other places.

Several legends surrounding the dogwood are still repeated in North Carolina. This is my cherished legend. One popular story holds that 2000 years ago the flowering dogwood tree stood straight and tall. Because the tree had such strong wood, the Roman soldiers under Pontius Pilate chose to make the cross of Jesus Christ out of the dogwood trunks. The dogwood tree was horrified but it had no choice. In order never to serve as a cross again, the dogwood became a slender twisted tree. In addition, to help people remember Jesus' sacrifice, the dogwood flower blooms in the spring in the shape of a cross with nail holes in the ends.

The dogwood is my favorite among the flowering trees. After buying, planting, and losing several dogwood trees, I decided to research how to grow and take care of them.

When my husband Preston and I moved to North Carolina, I just knew there would be dogwood trees everywhere since they grew wild. After walking and searching all of our three acres of property, not one was found. My heart was so broken, I cried. Silly, I know, but I had had my mind made up to find a dogwood on our own land.

A few days had gone by without me thinking of a dogwood tree. While washing the morning dishes, and looking out my kitchen window, what do my eyes see? There stood a wild dogwood tree in front of me! Where the woods meet the edge of the yard, a tall dogwood with blossoms was blooming high in a canopy of white. My heart jumped for joy at the sight.

Oh, Father God, thank You for one dogwood tree. One was all I needed to make me happy.

Now plans were made to show off this tree at the edge of the woods. I made a call to the North Carolina Extension Office to ask when was the proper time to trim my tree. To my surprise, the report to me was to not trim wild dogwoods; just leave them where they grow.

In that case, clearing the underbrush and debris from around the base of the tree would be the best thing to be done and that is exactly

what happened! Planting a ring of daylilies finished the project. There it was: God's masterpiece on display for all to see.

Now, in our home in Hudson, there is another magnificent white flowering dogwood tree. This one was purchased from a nursery as a sapling in Collettsville, North Carolina. Friends came over to our house to help with the transplanting of our new arrival. Shovels, gloves, tree potting soil, and the water hose were laid out on the place where this baby tree was to have a new home. Snacks, drinks, and other refreshments were served at the end of the day to celebrate the planting of the tree.

This happened twenty-five years ago. My heart is still joyful when I look out my kitchen window and see the radiant white flowers of the dogwood tree.

In the Woods
by
Thomas Blanton

I'm sitting in the woods on a rotting log.
The rotting log from a tree that fell years ago.
Years ago, this patch of woods covered more ground.
But more ground was needed for a garden.
The garden isn't there anymore so now it's a yard.
Another yard lies between the woods and my home.
My home's lot includes two patches of woods.
One patch of woods in front of the house and one behind it.
The one behind it is where I'm sitting.
Sitting here just watching my grandchildren play.
Watching grandchildren play is the best part of retirement.

The Old Walnut Tree
by
Gretchen Griffith

Grandpa stomped the mud from his shoes. "Hit's gonna be a wild 'un," he told Grandma as he hung his flannel shirt on the peg by the door to dry. "It's a howling wolf out there," she agreed. "Rain and wind make a dangerous mix. Best we sit tight and eat some of my fresh black walnut cake while we wait. Still warm." She set a slice of pound cake before him, its crumbs littering the red and white checkered oilcloth. Grandpa pinched them between his fingers and popped them in his mouth. How could he resist this from his bride of sixty years?

Although, if ever they argued, it was over the black walnut tree that made this cake possible. Her peace offering was a cake she baked at least once a month, and twice if there was a covered dish at the fellowship hall or if someone died. No funeral was proper without Essie's cake. Yes, sir, he knew how to rile her. Mention cutting that tree. Mention his one desire, one unmet goal in life. Mention crafting a fiddle from that old tree and the hackles on her neck would rise taller than a cat's fighting fur.

His belly full, he reached for the fiddle his own pappy had crafted years before. He drew the bow over the strings and began a mournful wail that seemed to match the skies above them that had darkened to near black of night. The water drummed against the windows, and the wind pulsed its rhythm: in, out, in, out. The side door banged a forlorn rhythm of its own as Grandpa lowered the fiddle. "Maybe we ought to go to the root cellar," he shouted above the roar.

Fiddle still in hand, he led her as they wound their way down the steps to the cellar. They huddled together, listening to the wind above them, and when the deafening crash boomed, they held each other tighter than ever before. In actuality, the tempest lasted perhaps less than half an hour. In fear time, it was hours upon hours before they gathered their wits about them to venture up the steps and see what the future held for them.

Panes on the side window were now shards on the floor. "Careful," he warned his wife. He held her hand as they edged their way through the kitchen to the back entrance. Grandma saw it first and gasped. "My tree." They stepped on the porch together.

"I'm sorry." He put his arm around her shoulder.

She pulled away. "I hope you're satisfied. Whatever will I do now?"

He stood helpless, his silence broken only by chainsaws in the distance. He faced her and leaned in. "You know I love you beyond any tree in the world. Right?"

She mustered a grin and whispered, "Right." They pecked a kiss and sighed a weary sigh. Then she added, "I'll find some work gloves if you'll go fetch the wheelbarrow."

Two weeks and two sore backs later, Grandpa finally started crafting his walnut fiddle. His pappy was a luthier and had taught him the bits of the trade as well, watching the walnut tree grow in the side yard of what was then his house. "It'll make a fine fiddle for sure, one day. Walnut makes a mellow tone. It'll be ready by the time you're an old man. You wait. The day will come."

Grandpa selected the perfect slice of wood from the downed tree. He cut it to a pattern and planed its innards to an angle that would balance sound as his pappy had taught him, if he remembered it correctly. He designed the f-shaped sound holes. He soaked thin strips to bend them and form sides. He sanded and polished it to showcase the natural beauty of the grain. He added the finishing necessities, the scroll head and neck, the pegs and strings.

In secret, he sanded two sticks from the tree, about a foot in length, pencil width, tapering to a dull point. Those were for his bride, not much of a replacement for the bushels of walnuts, but from his heart.

When he completed his fiddle and called her into the workshop to view his handiwork, he presented the sticks to her. "Fiddlesticks," he added when she hesitated.

"What?"

"That's what they are. They're fiddlesticks."

She studied them and then stared at him with one eyebrow cocked. A giggle slid from between her clenched lips. "Oh, my."

"They're for you to play on the fiddle. Like this." He demonstrated by tapping them on the strings. "Hear that? What do you think?" he asked when he finished.

She wiped away tears from her eyes. "Oh my," she stammered again. She threw her arms around her husband and her giggles escalated into riotous laughter.

"Well, fiddlesticks to that." Grandpa joined in her laughter.

"No! No! I think this is the most perfect gift ever! Thank you."

"There might not be any more black walnut pound cake, but there'll be some fine music from here on out." Grandpa handed the sticks to her as he picked up his brand new black walnut fiddle and began playing. He leaned toward her and invited her to join him in their first duet.

Master Closet
by
Linda McLaughlin LaRose

The moon stepped out of her fir,
Tried on the blue silk star-sequined sky
Then wrapped herself in the black lace
Of leafless branches.
She bared one white shoulder at her reflection
In the silver surface of the lake,
Slowly stepped over her garments,
Left scattered on the floor of the heavens
And said—"Clearly, I have nothing to wear."

Falls Positive
by
Stefanie Hutcheson

It's only a waterfall. Truthfully? It's man-made but it is outside so technically it counts as nature. Right? I mean, it doesn't stand there and issue a spoiler alert to let its many visitors know it isn't "real." It still compels, gently commands, and invites one to appreciate it.

Many do. Almost every time I pay homage to the Moravian Falls, I am not alone. Men go there and eat their lunch, basking across  the road from its gentle melody. Sightseers gape in wonder and look around, hoping someone will come along to take a picture of them with this majesty behind them. Though the area is roped off, it is not uncommon to see someone meandering down to the base. Some even dare to dip their tootsies in the cool waters.

For folks who love nature but prefer it from the sanctity of the inside of a car or a Pretty Purple Room window (trust me on this one: no bugs!!), this lovely area of interest happily obliges. One does not have to leave the security of a vehicle to enjoy. If the timing is right, no cars will be traveling and one can sit on the bridge and snap all the photos (selfies are a bit tough to navigate but can be taken with just the right amount of finesse) and listen to the dulcet rhythm of the cascading waters. And if a car does happen by? Usually it's a local driver who is used to this sort of frivolity. Ignore their smirks and remind yourself that you took the time to stop and smell the roses.

There's a hiking trail for those who aren't confined to their cars. It winds up a moderately strenuous trail. At the top, the beginning of the falls is seen, exhibiting a different sort of awareness of the wonders of God before man stepped in to try to improve His original design.

Moravian Falls, located in Wilkes County off of Hwy 18, is one of my happy places. When I need to get in touch with nature without nature touching too much of me, these falls are near the top of my list!

Value
by
Michael (MJ) FitzGerald

So, maybe there is some value to this thing. Just for the record, I am referring to the value of a tree here and not whatever pursuit of happiness you may have had in mind.

First off, let's look at the numbers. America is fourth in the world in forest resources, after the Russian Federation (Siberia is a *big* place), Brazil, and Canada. North Carolina is among the top ten states in forestry, with over 18 million acres of woodlands, or 60% of North Carolina's total land use. This means NC's forests cover more area than the state's pasture, farmland, and urban areas combined. There are approximately 300,000 private property owners on these forested acres. The owner of the most forest land is likely (no surprise) Weyerhaeuser, the large forest products firm, at 570,000 acres.

Our state also encompasses over a million total acres in four National Forests. The largest of these, Pisgah NF, with over 500,000 acres - much of which is in the Foothills - straddles the scenic Blue Ridge Parkway and borders the Great Smoky Mountains National Park. On a city level, Charlotte's civic leaders often refer to the community as a "City of Trees," increasing its park property despite continual pressure from business growth and residential development. Charlotte's natural tree canopy and forest habitat, however, have diminished in recent years. Now the number of grand oaks, elms, shady maples, and swaying pines hovers in the low forties percent of land use. For this reason, the city has become a leader in tree canopy sustainment initiatives and, like George Vanderbilt did years ago in Asheville, has hired arborists to survey and develop preservation plans.

Trees, Monetized
Enough of size. What is the value of all these trees? Surely, from an economics standpoint, we are dealing with (beneath?) imprecise standing timber estimates. There are fairly concrete business numbers, however. Pre-pandemic, in 2019, the forest sector in North Carolina directly contributed $21.6 billion in industry output to the state's economy. The forest sector - including forestry and logging operations,

sawmills, furniture mills, and pulp and paper industries - contributed, with the indirect and induced economic effects considered, $34.9 billion in industry output to North Carolina's business activities, generating more than 148,000 full- and part-time jobs with a payroll well over $8 billion. A decade ago, 18% of all timberland was artificially planted, primarily loblolly (*Pinus taeda*) pine, and, with increased demand, has likely increased substantially since then. Likewise, since the COVID pandemic's "pent-up demand" of 2020 and 2021, the forest sector's industry output - while the detailed statistics are not readily available just yet - has probably expanded.

For several years now, the 850 growers of Fraser (*Abies fraseri*) Firs have sustained North Carolina's ranking as the second state in the nation in providing America's Christmas trees. These trees are nurtured on 38,000 acres in fourteen different counties, with the Fraser species accounting for 94% of Christmas trees grown in North Carolina.

Stepping back from the details of North Carolina and Foothills economics - to see "the forest for the trees," if you will - the USDA *estimated*, in 2016, North Carolina's forests had 14.47 billion trees. Best Management Practices in forestry have likely increased this number since then, but if an entity were to attempt monetizing this natural resource, it would be quantified as 40.89 billion board feet.

Trees, Where We Tread

When we pivot from quantitative to qualitative, trees are, in essence, integral to our nature. Whether it is Eden in *The Bible*'s Genesis or Darwin's *Origin of the Species* (not mutually exclusive), humans have had trees in their experience almost since their awareness. How are we to package their value?

Scenically, trees span from grandeur to shrubs. In a virtual panic age of climate, they are harvested by the square miles in once-remote global rainforests. Beyond their ecosphere of carbon dioxide and oxygen exchange, they are home to critters of all descriptions - microbial, insects, slithery reptiles, birds, and mammals. Their shade alone harbors earthbound creatures and botanical wonders.

The seemingly endless variety of such characteristics of sizes and shapes of trunks, branches, and leaves, twigs, and buds, color and texture, flowers and fruit render the typical passerby either dismissive or mesmerized; one, withdrawn from nature's complexity, even ignoring birdsong; the other, fascinated with the forest's intricate detail.

Trees are so marvelous, yet so ordinary, to our existence. We typically take them for granted. Here in North Carolina, they recede into the common panorama. While intuitively enjoyed as we pass through our everyday life, unless we pause to enjoy a forest setting or a ridgeline's contours, the experience will not command our attention. Trees are not nearly as dramatic to us as they would be, say, to a cattleman out west approaching the Platte River, or a warrior of yesteryear scanning the horizon for buffalo. A tree's intrinsic value can not be measured, whether the beholder is Blue Ridge born and bred or a shepherd emerging from the desert.

References

Data extracted, 04/09/2022, from Economic Contribution of the Forest Sector in North Carolina, 2019 | NC State Extension Publications.

Data extracted, 04/09/2022, from https://content.ces.ncsu.edu/north-carolinas-forest-and-forest-products-industry-by-the-numbers

Data extracted, 04/09/2022, from https://ncchristmastrees.com/our-story/our-mission./

Pine Trees
by
Carol Starr

As a small child in Northern Canada, I never saw trees taller than twenty feet. Imagine my surprise when we moved south and I saw trees taller than houses.

In 2007, my husband Elliott and I bought a newly constructed house in the Foothills of North Carolina. The lot did not even have a blade of grass. So I planted grass and trees–thirty of them. Some trees didn't make it, but the maples, redbuds, and dogwoods did fine. A flowering cherry now dominates the front yard and is covered in fragrant white blossoms in April.

But I missed the red pines that towered over my father's lake cottage further south in Ontario.

So when the Caldwell County Cooperative Extension had a plant sale, I bought a bundle of six tiny white pine sprigs for $8.00. I planted them on the north side of the property. To my delight, all but one of them took hold. Through the years they slowly but steadfastly grew, filling the air with the pine scent I knew so well.

Usually in the spring, bluebirds raise a family in either of the birdhouses I put on two of the trunks.

One tree looms over the deck near the dining room. Squirrels love it. So do the goldfinches, Carolina wrens, house sparrows, and cardinals which flock to the birdfeeder just under the pine branches. Woodpeckers hammer out pests in any dead branches, helping the trees to stay healthy. Even the dog lounges in its generous shade.

I am amazed at how massive the trees have become. They dominate the north end of the backyard. I am so grateful to have

32

these lovely trees spreading their soft feathery needles over my special piece of heaven.

Veronicas
by
Kathy Lyday

April is the time of year when the fresh green domes of chartreuse leaves appear in the garden. My veronicas are emerging from their winter dormancy. I planted these lovely perennials four years ago and I look forward to their bright presentation each summer. Veronicas come in many colors but I have eight purple ones which bloom in thick clumps of spires. Requiring six to eight hours of sun per day, veronicas are considered pollinators because they attract butterflies and bees.

The bees sleep in the veronicas so they can start breakfasting as soon as the temperature hits sixty-two degrees. Collecting the pollen in sacs on their back legs, then moving from plant to plant, bees fertilize other receptive species. People are amazed at the number of bees the

veronicas attract. Several species of bees feast on the nectar from the veronicas, though most are bumblebees. Since there has been an extensive amount of weed killer applied in our community, honeybees are scarcer now, though we do have a few from time to time. Trying to count them is nearly impossible, but fun to attempt. My dog tries to eat the bees and will stalk them for hours. It tires him out as much as a long run.

It is fascinating to observe the bees stripping the flowers from the bottom of the spire up to the top–leaving nothing in between. Once the bees clean a spire completely, they start at the bottom of another one; they do not feed haphazardly. Bees are tidy creatures. They do what my hairdresser advises: go from roots to ends.

Also known as Speedwell, veronicas will grow from three feet in height up to two feet across. They have to be staked due to their heavy blooms. They are drought-tolerant and do well as long as they get sufficient light. As fall approaches, I cut off the branches that have been stripped but leave every half-eaten spire until all the purple has disappeared. When the color is gone, the bees are too. Same time next year...I hope.

Seasons, Holidays, and Traditions

Snowfall Sentinels
by
Steve Downing

In preparation for winter holidays – with hopes of a "White Christmas" – my family positions a small plastic gnome on the deck's picnic table to stand watch and measure the amount of snowfall.

Our daughters and grandchildren also carry on the tradition – although Troll Dolls are their preferred sentinels.

'Da Snow Gnome' is about eight inches tall. If the white fluffy stuff buries him up to his belly, there is enough snow to make snow cream.

Snow cream! Yum!!

Yah, I know… I hear native North Carolinians objecting: "The first snowfall cleanses the air. You wait for the second snowfall to make snow cream."

"Poppycock," I say. As a transplant to the Foothills and a former science teacher, I know that in order for water vapor to condense in the atmosphere it needs a dust particle to glom onto. The air is never totally clean!

So, a bowl full of fresh powder mixed with several spoonfuls of Borden's Eagle Brand sweetened condensed milk and all of it whisked together… Voila`! Best instant ice cream ever!

This year Da Snow Gnome went missing. Normally he relaxes in the basement for three-quarters of the year. Couldn't find him when I went looking just before Thanksgiving.

I drafted two new figurines to stand watch: Sno Cat and Kit.

After the first snowfall (and snow cream), Da Snow Gnome emerged to assume duty with Sno Cat and Kit. He now stands proudly with them, hoping for a late February or early March snowfall.

FYI:

Da Snow Gnome spent his off-duty time snuggled in a basket of fuzzy stuffed animals. He's such a flirt! No wonder we couldn't find him this past November…

Dog Bingo
by
Kathy Lyday

I bought it on sale at T.J. Maxx. My intention had been to use it as a gift for the "Dirty Santa" exchange at our dog obedience club Christmas party, but for some reason, I could not give this one away. It went into the cabinet, and months later I ran across it while looking for Easter decorations.

Dog Bingo comes in a white square box with labeled pictures of dogs on it. The box contains a foldable board picturing sixty-four dog breeds in alphabetical order. There are individual dog tokens that the caller draws and places on the large board. Players choose a card featuring twenty-five pictured dog breeds and receive several royal blue cardboard circles to mark the breeds called. It is just like regular bingo.

My family came for Easter dinner, and I thought it would be fun to play Dog Bingo afterward. When I presented the suggestion, my daughters exchanged a look which indicated I needed a psychiatric evaluation. "Just try it," I pleaded. So, after all of the dishes were done, we started Dog Bingo.

I called out the names of the dogs on the tokens I drew, showed the pictures, and placed them on the large board. There were well-known dogs like Golden Retrievers and Boxers, but also the Affenpinschers and the Briards, which required a second look. Not everyone could conjure up the image of a Kooikerhondje, so it helped to see what cards had been drawn. The rule brochure also included facts about each of the breeds. We consulted that frequently when an unknown dog token surfaced.

I looked around the table; the players were engaged. My daughters and sons-in-law helped one another, making sure that everything was marked. They hurried me along--"Ok, what's the next one?" They high-fived when two of them had the same dog and peeked at each other's cards to see who was close to a bingo. When someone's card got knocked over, everyone helped to recreate it. The suspense built until all four of them needed just one dog to call bingo. My oldest daughter won with the Blackmouth Cur on a diagonal.

"Do you want to play again," I asked? They all did. And we played again and again until I was hoarse from shouting out Dandie Dinmont Terrier multiple times. Did I mention that there were prizes? I had a basket prepared that contained everything from Almond Joy candy bars to Jimmy John's gift cards.

They liked the prizes, but they liked the game even more. There was no skill necessary; no strategizing or creativity required. It was a screen-free reality break. Watching almost forty-somethings become engrossed in this simple game was delightful. My mind ran back to the sweet old days of Candyland and Operation.

After that Easter, we started to play the game at other family gatherings. I have even introduced Dog Bingo to some of my friends, and we played at my house. Although they enjoyed it and we laughed a lot, it wasn't the same as with the kids. One intriguing facet of Dog Bingo is rarely does the same person win multiple times. Surprisingly, almost every player gets a chance at victory. I would *love* to know how this magic happens.

My family has not been together as much during the Pandemic, and we have not played Dog Bingo in a couple of years. Noticing it on the shelf the other day, I wondered if they had forgotten about it.

Since my daughters are establishing traditions of their own, my youngest invited me to her house for Christmas. She had decorated the house and bought matching pajamas for everyone. She called and we talked about how I could help. She thought for a minute and then asked, "Mom, would you please bring Dog Bingo?"

Jake and the Christmas Trail
by
Gretchen Griffith

The first text arrived at 3:58 pm. "We can't find Jake anywhere." I reread the message on the screen and cringed. As the pageant coordinator, it was up to me to handle last-minute actor substitutions, but how could I replace a donkey at this late hour?

For over two decades, Littlejohn United Methodist, the church I attend here in the Foothills, has presented an outdoor drama about the birth of Jesus. The audience walks in small groups following the "Christmas Trail" through the woods at our church park. A guide directs them from one scene to the next as the story unfolds through a variety of Josephs, Marys, and other Biblical characters.

For almost that many years, Jake, the donkey, has had the privilege of bringing Mary to the inn. Children who later knelt with the shepherds at the manger first oohed and aahed at the sight of Mary perched on his furry back. He performed, and we rewarded him. He ate his treats, and his belly filled. When the evenings ended, he loaded back onto the trailer and returned to his pasture.

Two nights of the trail that year had already gone well. Actors performed brilliantly, and only one replacement was needed for a guide who had laryngitis on that particular Saturday night. As a go-to troubleshooter, I turned my attention to more pressing activities while the support personnel around me performed their assigned tasks. Actors began dressing in costumes. The bonfire at the end of the trail was lit. The water for the hot chocolate boiled on the camp stoves. All was moving along like clockwork. All except Jake.

There was still time before the first group started on the trail at half past six. I wasn't worried. As I waited in the cold for a Jake update, I put myself in his shoes…hooves. I pictured him minding his own donkey business in the field, chomping on stubble, warding off coyotes, braying his opinions every so often, and then hearing the clunk of the horse trailer. He probably knew exactly what that meant. Being led down a cleared path in the woods. Waiting patiently for an innkeeper to send this couple on their way. Repeating his part in the scene nearly twenty times during the evening with carrots as his reward.

How could we continue without Jake? When asked what they enjoyed most about the trail, children almost always said "the donkey." Jake was the star of the show in their minds. In the wonder of a chilly walk through the woods, baby Jesus in the manger came in a distant second.

A second text chimed with less than an hour to go and darkness falling. "Never did find that donkey." The last they had seen him, I found out later, he had taken off to the far corner of the pasture to hide in a section covered in scrubby tangles of underbrush. The search for him had to be suspended, not only because of the tight schedule, but also for safety purposes.

The word *absconded* came into my mind. He didn't know the word, but he lived the definition – to depart secretly and hide. Why did he pick the most popular night of the pageant to be stubborn like a donkey? Without Jake, Mary and Joseph had no choice but to walk, so I sent a message to our costume director in case she needed to adjust their clothing.

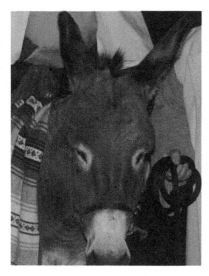

Only later did I have time to reflect about Jake's stubborn refusal to work that night. We only asked him to do one chore, follow Joseph. He failed us. He failed those children who came through the trail. He went off in the other direction and had no intention whatsoever of doing our will.

Something strange happened to me, and I confess it now. I realized I was a tiny bit jealous of that donkey and his freedom to abscond. For a fleeting moment I wished I could have had the nerve, and like Jake, escape pressures of the myriad of duties weighing on my back.

I'll never know what logic went through Jake's mind leading to his decision to bolt that one night. He was back in his place by the next performance. Go figure. But what I do know is that with the focus away from a donkey, Jesus became what the children spoke of most as they warmed themselves around the fire. As it should be.

Winter Spring Summer Fall
by
Carol Starr

In the winter months
It's cool you'll need a sweater
And some nice warm socks

In the spring months
It's tricky so be prepared
Boots, sneakers, flip flops

In the summer months
Bright sunshine and thunderstorms
Hot days muggy nights

In the fall months
The leaves crunch beneath your feet
Campfires, soup, blankies

The Fall
by
Linda McLaughlin LaRose

Trees perform their striptease—
We can't look away or we'll miss
The last of the graceful leaves,
When limbs all bare and bold
Against the sun going down
Hold on to the last chance of light
That draws a shadow curtain
To frame the moon at center stage
For a second act. So we stay,
And you say, "Where were you then,
When I was young and wondering?"
Even so, we never say "What if…,"
Nor regret the seasons of our lives.
Spring was for offspring, seeds sown
Now view us stripped and disowned
When we all fall down, broken by love.
We go inside. Light the fire. Ask for grace.
Winter, wait for us. We are coming.

Christmas Fireworks
by
Thomas Blanton

When I was growing up we never shot off fireworks for the Fourth of July. Our fireworks holiday was Christmas. Every year in early December, my father and I would go to South Carolina, where firecrackers were legal, and bring a bagful home: sparklers, Roman Candles, skyrockets, M-80s, Cherry Bombs, etc. We would celebrate during the Christmas vacation by shooting these fireworks off.

One Christmas Eve, my family and I came home from celebrating with my mom's folks to find a burning stump in the driveway between our house and my aunt's house next door. When we got out of the car and walked over to investigate, my cousins appeared out of the shadows. They had seen our car lights and had hidden for fear that the car they saw might be a law enforcement officer since they were lighting firecrackers on that stump. So we hung around to help them shoot more fireworks off. It was a memorable Christmas Eve that year. We shot more fireworks than usual, which is saying something since we normally spent a considerable sum at the South Carolina fireworks stores.

The Christmas fireworks tradition in our family goes back a long way. My grandfather was in charge of the county roads in the first part of the Twentieth Century, so he had access to dynamite. He walked along the road on Christmas Eve, lighting a stick of dynamite every little bit and throwing it to the side.

Every Christmas found us celebrating the birth of Christ with a bang – a bunch of bangs accompanied by the bright lights of Roman Candles, the glow of sparklers, and the brilliance of soaring skyrockets.

Now, that was really some Christmas fireworks.

Summer's Finest
by
Stefanie Hutcheson

Sunflowers. Glorious, bright, wonderful sunflowers. How I love them!

Each year, my husband Steve digs me up a patch or two (sometimes three!) of ground in the backyard and/or along the driveway. Carefully he places the tiny little seeds of promise and I anxiously await the time when the green shoots start appearing.

Through the summer, I watch with happiness as they stretch their limbs upwards and their leaves reveal tiny little heads of expectations. As the heads expand and slowly open, my heart sings! I cannot explain why but these bright flowers seem to encourage me. They bear up under the heat. A bit of tending to--such as removing weeds--and they thrive. They rely on the sun for their needs and the Son provides mightily. Watering when they need it, sending the winds to strengthen them, the Master Gardener uses these stalks of sunshine to warm my tired soul.

Not only do they offer me food for the soul, but they also provide for the fowls of the air. One summer a couple of years ago, they were extra spectacular. The butterflies flocked to them and the bees happily hummed. The pictures I took of them were shared daily as others vicariously enjoyed their beauty. See for yourself!

Ahh, sunflowers. God's gift to His kids. How I treasure You!

45

In Search of the Elusive Christmas Tree
by
Lucy Wilkes

The winter season in the Foothills brings about a beauty of its own. The leaves are gone revealing the landscape. The evergreens show life is still here. Oh, yes, the holidays of Thanksgiving and Christmas are near. A nip on the nose, a shiver from the cold, brought a hope for a chance of a small snow.

Since we have two grandsons, the tradition of picking out the perfect Christmas tree was the highlight of the season. Driving up Highway 181 North near the Blue Ridge Parkway, where the Christmas tree nurseries are located, became an adventure in itself. Winding roads, the anticipation of the sight of a snowflake, and of course, singing Christmas carols added to the excitement.

Arriving at the nursery, running to the store where hot apple cider was being served, added to the completion of the plan. Back outside, jumping in the open-air wagon with other joyful riders, the trip up the hill was rough and rocky, adding to the thrill.

Ascending past the smaller trees, the smell of pine filled the air as the boys waited anxiously to be there. To unload, to run, and to search for that perfect tree was more than they could bear. The boys began looking, hunting, and peeking around the trees. Finally, there it was! The perfect glorious Christmas Tree. Now that it was found, the workers cut it, wrapped it, and sent it down to the store. Yes indeed, the elusive perfect Christmas tree was captured once more.

Back home, we set up and decorated with lights, and ornaments with memories of the past. It was ready to be put on display for Thanksgiving and Christmas Day.

In the Seasons, Traditions, and Holidays in the Foothills, there are opportunities to bring families and friends together to celebrate with each other.

Midnight Confessions

Letter to Lizbeth That Will Never Be Mailed
by
Linda McLaughlin LaRose

Dear Lizbeth,

Here's a letter that will never be mailed. Some day you will know why. We are back home in the mountains now, and I miss all your shenanigans and goings-on about town. This wasn't how I planned it. I was going to take responsibility for my actions just as soon as I got the girls settled, only there is a problem. Glory B has lost her voice and needs help of a kind I can't give her, I have contacted someone in Columbia to see if hypnosis can break down the wall she has built up. There is nothing wrong with her throat or vocal cords, but something in her mind, and I miss my girl even when she is sitting right there at the same table, or we are in front of the fire together No tinctures, no yarrow tea, nothing has worked, and I am at my wit's end. Never felt so helpless since she was a baby and her mama and daddy both out of the picture. Thanks to you, we made it through that long spell of hard luck and heartbreak.

You are always on my mind now that I know our friendship will end. I am sorrier than I can ever say. But I try to focus on what is right in front of me, like the trees up here have changed color. Look out this window at the mountains and it's like party dresses flung across a great big featherbed, and us like children allowed to stay up and watch. After dark there is Coondog making a racket chasing something and howling that song he sings all night long, making me think he hails from these hills himself, just so happy. Half the population calls me "Ma'am" and the other half calls me "Little Missy," and me a great-grandma!

Here you can watch the sunrise several times in succession of a morning when you wind 'round a road on an uphill climb. In the mountains next to a hill with hidden sapphires my dead husband swore were the size of his fist and just as hard, though he was tender with me, it's no wonder the blueberry bushes still sit in their cans, ground so rocky you can't dig a hole to bury a cat, so this is not a good place for a grave digger. I shouldn't mention graves here in this letter to you, but I stopped by the graveyard to pay respect. The preacher says he has to

48

pinch pennies so hard they squeak, and it's hardly worth passing the offering plate. I couldn't bring myself to tell him what was on my mind.

But I believe redemption is real, and changing water into wine or raising the dead, well, that was small potatoes compared to the pressure-washing power of Jesus to create this clean heart. I am a work in progress. He is not done with me, not yet. Sometimes I put up one heckuva of a fight. I will get back to that directly. Rose is here, making a tent with sheets draped over the tabletop and I want to think about the good things, count my blessings, and she is at the top of that list.

I keep thinking about gardens, or fishing, or carpentry because on the ride up here a revelation occurred in which I was shown The Way, and though it was laid out before me in a lifetime of sermons and Sundays, it never spoke so directly or clearly to me as it does now. It says to me, "Do this. Now. Yes, you. Grow food. Fish for your supper. Build something." We were put here on this earth, and we were put in a garden, and told not to eat of the fruit. I try to find the lessons where I can, but my decision and actions force me to defy this urge that has come upon me. I am in a spiritual quandary, but I intend to follow my plan of action and come clean soon as I know Glory will make it without me.

All I ever wanted was to do the right thing, the loving thing, but sometimes you don't have much of a choice. Loving my neighbor has always come natural for me, but I forgot to take care of myself. Now I'm old, I have afflictions, and they say I'm hardheaded, or I might have seen the light sooner. I have entertained pain, but I was not a good hostess, letting doctors have their way with me for far too long before I began to trust my own instincts, what the old ones taught me, and the plants that grew free. I have lived a life, and come what may, I will die someday. But let me not die without doing all I can for them, my people.

These are things I thought about this evening while sewing curtains on the old Singer, pushing out other thoughts, like how Susannah up and died leaving a world of fabric and a baby girl. Now that baby girl is all grown up, with her own baby girl and they are both going to be free from prying eyes when I hang up these curtains in all the colors Susannah chose years ago, reminding us that life is precious, maybe even a bargain. Glory has dipped into her mother's stash so many times, designing little dresses and pinafores to sell and help make ends meet.

49

Rose was in her own little heaven today, playing outside, and the bees wove in and out of her red hair bumping into each other like drunks at a party, and her not the least bit scared, as if she was a real rose. Glory will find the hive and soon have boxes abuzz with honey. She has a gift for the beekeeping, a true bee charmer.

Well, I've rambled enough and it's time to get supper on, but I'm here to tell you—I just got started good. Something just died outside. I heard it screaming. Makes me shiver to remember—but he didn't suffer—not like that, I can tell you for a fact. I can't say any more, but I will, soon.

I am back in the mountains, I don't know what will come of me. These hills are wild. This life is real. It will be a struggle, but once I get the girls set up, I will go back and face what's ahead. Glory will be free and clear. It's all on my head, ever bit of it. Her daddy will have to step up and take over, no use pretending. It's time. As for me and what I done, I can't ask for forgiveness, only mercy.

I am sorrier than you will ever know.

Much love,

Ida Claire

An Odd Sunday Dream
by
Carol Starr

I woke up Monday morning in the midst of an interesting dream. I was in a large building that had an auditorium. They were having a graduation ceremony for men. The graduation ceremony for women was to be held later.

Outside the auditorium near the stage, there was a woman who was huddled down with only the gray clothes she was wearing and a blanket. I sensed that she was here to receive a diploma. Every time the announcer called a name that started with "G," the woman walked onto the stage. People chuckled because she was a woman, not a man.

I tried to talk to her but she just looked puzzled. I asked her if she spoke English. She didn't understand me. Finally, I said "Kan du tala svenska?" (Can you speak Swedish?) It was the only Swedish I knew. (My mother was Swedish but had never learned how to speak the language.)

The woman nodded her head "yes." I knew this silent person, although able to speak, was rational and harmless.

I carried her throughout the building, asking people, "Does anyone speak Swedish?" One woman said she spoke a little Swedish, but she was in a classroom taking an exam and was not allowed to take time to help.

In one room, a staff member was taking a tray of food to a patient in a hospital bed. I wondered if this woman had eaten anything.

I knew two or three friends, including a young man, who did speak Swedish, but I did not know how to contact them at the moment.

I awoke wondering: Who was this patient woman? How did she earn a diploma if she couldn't speak English? What was she doing here? Why was I carrying her? Why did I know she spoke Swedish?

Is He a Po'boy?
by
Michael (MJ) FitzGerald

Billy had a crush on Sally Stryker for as long as he could remember. He reckoned it could never be, though, since his dad ran off the road one night, killing himself and another woman.

Billy's Uncle Chet figured he'd been out showing his new friend his latest still and they had both sampled too much of the wares. Forensics showed that much conclusively. That had been three years ago, and that front-page story had pretty much sealed the deal far as Billy's chances to win Sally.

Chances had been slim anyway since Billy's folks were a long way from Sally's entrepreneurial, country club parents. His mom managed the old Golden Rest 24-room motel on the edge of town, having worked her way up from being a dependable person on the cleaning crew for several years. His dad, however, was a feast or famine character, landing good-paying jobs for his truck and Bobcat, or squandering his income and savings by investing in wine, women, and song. Kind by nature, but worthless as a planner, his latest moonshine venture had followed scams of sports-based betting pools and regular, unfortunate sessions of backroom poker games. In short, Billy's dad was not greatly missed, beyond his children and a few ne'er-do-well friends. The townspeople generally saw his end as "reaping what he had sown."

Billy's family promptly sold his father's equipment so Billy could finish high school and learn a trade, if not go to college. Sally's family, meanwhile, bought her a condo next to campus in Boone so she could prepare herself to join the family's combined, yet separate, legal and venture capital firms. Her path was clear and she embraced it with typical enthusiasm. Any hint of attraction between high school seniors was snuffed out by the scandal of Billy's dad. No prom pairing was allowed or tolerated. Sympathy for the family's loss did not extend to involvement with the Stryker's only daughter.

No one could have seen then that bachelor Uncle Chet Winstead, Dad's only sibling and firstborn of the family, would succumb to a massive heart attack at forty-four. Everyone assumed he would "get caught" long before forty and would have a passel of children by then, but he had buckled down to his independent logging business and built it into the largest in the county.

Rather than deliberately courting a woman, Uncle Chet courted the forest. Pursuing Forest Service and Highway Department contracts, as well as hammering out custom exchanges of logging services for cleared lands, he had substantially added - through exchange or outright purchases - to Grandpa's steep timberlands just west of the South Mountains. Grandpa had long since passed, but not before a fistfight falling out when Billy's daddy was an adolescent. Grandpa sent his son off bleeding and bruised. All the while, Billy's dad (long before he met Billy's mom) was swearing and denying he would become a father, claiming he didn't know who the father was. Grandpa did not like his measure, then, of his second born, and never revised his decision. His property, all his property (he had worked all his life), went to his oldest son, Billy's Uncle Chet.

Now Chet had died suddenly and who would have guessed he had a will giving his entire estate (sparing a generous annual stipend to Billy's mom) to his favorite, and only, nephew! Grandpa was land rich and cash poor. Uncle Chet was land richer and cash comfortable, albeit with considerable business equipment and associated debt.

Billy would need a sharp probate lawyer to convert the estate's buildings, plant and equipment, and vehicles (its "non-liquid" collateral) into "paid off" debt obligations. When asked, his coach responded, "Who better to handle Chet's estate than Stryker & Stryker?"

Billy immediately thought of Sally's grandaddy's firm, and smiled.

Road Food
by
Kathy Lyday

I was teaching my dog, Oscar, to recycle and it wasn't going well. I would hand him the container that yesterday's chicken salad wrap came in and tell him to "bring it." We would go from the kitchen and then into the garage where I kept the gray recycling tote. If he got that far with the recyclable and didn't shake it around like prey or crush it with his paws, he would drop it beside the container, but it did not always land inside. The day before, he had successfully dropped a chicken broth carton and a graham cracker box straight into the tote and was handsomely rewarded with a jackpot of treats each time. I knew he could do it again if only he could focus. We needed a walk to clear our heads and regroup.

It had rained for a few days straight and it was already 87°F at 8:30 in the morning. I patted my pocket and realized I had forgotten to bring dog treats. Oh, please let us avoid any distractions.

We walked up the sidewalk and crossed the street. To the left was a driveway that led to a dumpster near the woods. We passed that and headed down the hill. We liked to go out of the Arbor Acres complex so Oscar could sniff. We headed down the sidewalk on a heavily traveled street in a suburban neighborhood– the same route we took every morning. The sidewalk bordered a field with two massive pin oaks. Queen Anne's lace and dandelions were blooming among the weeds. They mowed the field every so often and the flowers disappeared, but they never sprayed weed killer, so I liked to walk there. The area behind the field was densely wooded so we don't go down that far. Our route took us down the hill to the creek and then we turned around and retraced our steps.

The sidewalk was still wet, as was the grass. Oscar veered over to the side of the road where a gigantic mushroom sat under one of the pin oak trees. The rain must have caused it to spring up. He was pulling hard and the prong collar didn't make any difference. I could see it more clearly when we got to the trunk of the tree: it wasn't a mushroom. It was a cheesecake.

A whole cheesecake—intact, under a tree. There was no box or plate or cardboard circle; it was just sitting by itself on the ground. A bouncer at a motorcycle bar would have had a hard time keeping my seventy-two-pound lab from trying to gobble it. By the time I could get him back from it by pulling as hard as I could and yelling "leave it" in a gruff voice, he had eaten a good chunk of it.

This wasn't the first food that I had seen on the side of the road. A few times a week I would see a half-eaten sandwich, part of a biscuit, or even a bag of tater tots. But they were castoffs, never anything whole like the cheesecake.

The hill was fairly long, but it was interesting to me that random food always showed up just as the descent began. The skinny yellow "Beware Gas Pipeline" sign between the sidewalk and the street seemed to be the target.

Days passed and the cheesecake was still there. It must have been full of preservatives to have remained intact after being in the July heat for a week.

To Oscar's delight, people threw food out all the time, but why at exactly the same place? The cheesecake was on the grass and all of the other food was on the street. Did that mean that the cheesecake was thrown out from the passenger's side and the other food from the driver's side? Were the same people throwing it out? Were litterers just missing the mark, or hoping someone would pick up their trash and take it down to the dumpster?

I even wondered idly if someone's spouse had been monitoring their diet, and they were ridding themselves of cheating evidence before arriving home. Three days later, the cheesecake was gone. I was sure that all the neighborhood dogs had higher glucose levels by that time.

As we were taking a walk late one afternoon, Oscar wanted to head toward the dumpster. It was surrounded by brick on three sides with one side left open for access. On the portion opposite the opening, there was a huge fig bush whose leaves were curling in the heat.

As we drew nearer, I spotted a square white cardboard container on the ground under the fig--the kind that you never can figure out which side is supposed to be the top when adding your leftovers. Somebody must have missed the dumpster. Oscar sniffed the container and started gnawing on it as if to pick it up. He wanted to recycle!

Jubilant that our earlier recycling work had imprinted, I started to pick up the container, then realized how heavy it was. I opened it to find three massive fried chicken fingers sitting on a bed of fries. There were small containers of coleslaw, ketchup, and honey mustard tucked into three of the corners.

Oscar was jumping up to get the food. I did not know the source of it, so I threw it in the dumpster. "Sorry, buddy, this is not ours."

The next morning I read the following article on the front page of the local paper:

> *"Homeless family found in woods"*
> *Yesterday afternoon, local conservationists collecting trash in the woods behind Arbor Acres were surprised to discover a campsite, including a tent and a baby stroller. Hesitant to confront the inhabitants, the police were called in to make initial contact. The occupants were said to be homeless, but had just signed a lease on an apartment and were moving in the next day. Police will check the area after the 24-hour grace period.*

When I watched the news that evening, I found out more: a blonde reporter in a hot pink sleeveless dress was standing in front of the local soup kitchen covering the story. Apparently, neighbors who visited the soup kitchen had known about the couple living in the woods and were taking food and leaving it nearby for the family since they did not have transportation.

The reporter looked at the audience, smiled broadly, and gestured to the two men standing beside her. "I am here with Mr. Clem Lail and Mr. JW Keener. These gentlemen knew about the family living in the woods behind Arbor Acres and were sharing their own daily takeout plates with them."

She continued, "The police have confirmed that the family has already moved into their new apartment and left the wooded campsite in pristine condition."

"Mr. Lail," the reporter asked as she turned to Clem with the mic, "would you please tell us more about how you kept the family in the woods fed?"

Clem, an older gentleman wearing a black t-shirt and a green John Deere hat, put his hand on his chin and stroked an imaginary

56

beard. He motioned toward his friend, JW, a big guy with curly blond hair and a tattoo on his bicep that said "Bob's Burgers."

"Well, J Dubby and me, we would split a plate, and then we would git in his truck an' take the other plate over there and leave it under the big bush," he said. "Leastways they'd have a little sump'n. You know, cuz 'o that baby and all."

The reporter sounded like she needed an antihistamine when she continued, "Well, Mr. Keener, I know you must be happy that the family has found a permanent home." JW grinned, gave the reporter a big thumbs up, and replied, "I sure is!"

As I watched this I realized that *I* was the reason that the homeless family missed a meal. I did not sleep well that night.

Early the next morning I went over to the soup kitchen and talked to the director. I asked him if I could speak with Clem or JW. He said, "Sure, they'll be here between 10:30 and 11:00." So, I waited.

I saw them pull up in JW's once-white F150. I walked up to them, introduced myself, and said that I had seen them on the news and wanted to congratulate them on what they had done. I asked them to please give an envelope to the homeless family for me, and they assured me they would. I also slipped each of them a little cash for their trouble.

As I was about to leave, I asked, "Did you guys ever give the family any sweets or just 'real food'?" They both got tickled and laughed until Clem was bent over double. When they composed themselves, JW wiped his eyes and said, "We tried, but it disappeared!" Then Clem said, "We got 'em a cake and some sweet rolls the Sara Lee bakery was givin' out. It was dark and we was trying to get near the woods to leave 'em. We got to the spot and there weren't no cake. The box was plumb empty. We left the sweet rolls, though." They said they had gone back to look, but it was so dark they never could find the cake.

I had to ask. "Was it a cheesecake that you lost?" They looked at each other and Clem nodded. "I found it," I said, and told them the story. We all chuckled about that and I thanked them for sharing their story with me and left so they could get their meal.

Oscar and I still walk every day and we still find food on the road. Last week, I happened to see a pizza box under the fig tree. I quickly turned Oscar around, and we headed for home.

Shooting Mistletoe
by
Thomas Blanton

"You can park here," Randy said.

Bill pulled the truck to the edge of the woods.

"The mistletoe is right over there."

Bill got out of his truck and got his 20-gauge shotgun from behind the seat. Randy and his brother Chuck climbed out and the three boys started walking. They went about twenty yards into the woods.

Randy pointed to the treetop. "Up there."

The boys were the bass horn players in the high school band and they had been assigned to bring the mistletoe to the band's Christmas party the next night.

Bill shot into the mistletoe growth and several sprigs dropped to the forest floor. The other boys started picking them up.

Bill reloaded and shot again. More mistletoe sprigs fell.

Before Bill could reload again, bullets started zinging overhead.

They all looked up and around.

More bullets whizzed by. They all ducked.

"What's going on?" Chuck yelled.

"I'm gonna go find out," Bill said. "Wait here."

Bill reloaded and moved through the woods to the left of where the bullets were coming from. He crossed a ditch and climbed up the hill and found himself on a dirt driveway. He turned right and walked toward where he heard the shooting.

Around a curve, he came upon a boy about his age with a semi-automatic .22 rifle. Two other boys were standing with him. When he saw Bill, he stopped shooting.

"We were over there where you were shooting. You almost hit us."

The boy looked at Bill's gun in the crook of his arm and said, "I was shooting at you. Y'all are trespassing. You need to get out of our woods."

"Well, we didn't know we were trespassing. We were just shooting down some mistletoe. We'll leave when I get back there."

One of the other boys said, "Paul got this gun for Christmas and he's trying it out."

Paul took aim at a can lying by the driveway and plinked a few shots into it.

Bill pointed his shotgun and blew the can away. Then he reloaded while Paul and the other boys stared.

Paul squinted his eyes and looked at Bill. "I believe I could shoot you a couple of times before you got off a shot at me."

"Maybe so. But we don't want to find out, do we?"

Bill let Paul make a few more noises about shooting and let him shoot at a couple of cans more. Then Bill blasted another can Paul was shooting at and said, "We'll be going on now. We won't bother you anymore."

Paul didn't say anything, just stood there with his friends (relatives?), gripping his rifle, trying in vain to look menacing, so Bill went back the way he came.

When he got back to the other boys, they had dropped the mistletoe into the truck, had climbed in themselves, and were ready to leave.

As they were driving away, Randy said, "I had no idea anybody would care if we were there."

"Don't worry about it," Bill said. "I'm just glad I had my gun. Now, let's go decorate for that party."

His Name Was Bill
by
Stefanie Hutcheson

Mark? Jeff? I'm sure it was a four-letter name.

Bill. His name was Bill.

Bill! That's right! Mercy, how could I forget that?

Honestly, pretty easily. We only had one night together. One fun-filled, exciting, happy-go-lucky evening of adventure.

He was a football player and...how do I say this? Attractive, definitely. Sexy? Mmn, I guess. If you're into tall, blonde, blue-eyed hunks then sure. Bill *was* sexy. To most. And maybe in another place and at another time I might have fallen for him.

I tried.

I mean it: I really tried to want this guy. That night--especially--I needed a distraction and that was what Bill gave me.

Joe Jackson was singing "Breaking Us In Two." Yeah, Joe: I *did* feel like trying something new! Bill especially liked this song and many times through the years--even though his face is only a blur--I go back to Mars Hill College, the fall of 1982, my yellow station wagon, and a night of adventure.

Somehow he and I wound up together in an otherworldly jaunt. Whether his idea or mine, we thought it would be hilarious to trade the portraits hanging over the mantles of the women's dormitories for those of the men's formidable canvases in the--well, (pardon the pun) you get the picture.

I drove, backing my car as closely as possible to the steps, while Bill raced inside to remove the painting. Maybe there was another fella along with us. Yeah, probably so. Had to have been, for this was too much work--even for a stud like Bill.

Gingerly placing the treasure in the back, we raced to the next men's dorm, swapped out portraits, and then repeated the process until at least six important pillars of the college had new homes.

Did I mention that I was--for the most part--a good girl? As though in a trance, I watched myself being this crazy co-ed, fearing nothing from being caught. Proud of myself for getting some street cred, in innocent ignorance I blithely played my part in this prank and, of course, denied it all the next day.

To most.

The night wound down. Bill started to kiss me, and again, I tried. I really wanted to be…

Sigh.

I didn't know what I wanted to be. Who I wanted to be. Or with. But something inside told me it wasn't Bill. So (again please pardon the pun) after giving it the good ol' college try, I drove Bill back to his dorm. This time the kiss was on the cheek, a smile of slight regret in both of our eyes, and a one-night stand that ended before it began.

I can't recall Bill's last name. For some reason, he wasn't in the yearbook. Nor did he return for the spring semester. If I hadn't gone downstairs the next morning and seen Professor Claude Myers staring down at me where Ms. Edna Moore usually glared at me, I might have thought it had been a dream. Was the Prof looking at me with amusement? Did he even wink perhaps? Again, I can't recall. Nonetheless, as I exited the dormitory, I didn't look back.

Then.

But every once in a while? Ah, every once in a while, I sneak a peek back into my rebellious college days and nights, thank God for what I thought were unanswered prayers, and whisper a word of thanksgiving to Him for His mercies and Him knowing what and who I really needed. Kind of gives the song "Breaking Us In Two" a double entendre, don't you think?

A Ghost Tale of a Town
by
Lucy Wilkes

As the story begins I'm on the deck writing when a storm arrives. While I moved my tables, my laptop, and iced tea inside, the wind slammed the door shut. Oh! The door is locked! The thought crossed my mind. I turned to run downstairs to go through the garage door when the rain started to pour. It seems the ghosts of Mortimer, NC resent the legend being told.

Once I resettle for writing, the creativity wouldn't come. However, the sound of the gentle rain with no wind awakens my imagination again. Now the words will appear as we continue from here.

The ghost town is in the upper part of Wilson Creek Township, in Caldwell County, among the Foothills. As we embark on this adventure for the truth, remember the winner tells the story. We decide what is fact or fiction while we explore what happened so long ago.

The village seemed to spring up overnight and became a thriving community that produced lumber, textiles, and other manufactured goods. Guests would come from miles around to enjoy the entertainment at the Laurel Inn Hotel. One famous visitor was Theodore Roosevelt who had a dance with Mrs. Bill Mortimer and possibly snuck a kiss on the cheek. Imagine dancing with the President of the United States.

A train ride through peaceful mountains brought a sense of belonging to the minds of those who relaxed in their seats. At one time, eight hundred residents called this town home, since they worked for the mills.

That week I interviewed Marie Cook. As the story goes, Marie's grandmother, Martha Jones, was employed by the Laurel Inn Hotel as a supervisor over the kitchen and housekeeping. I heard she reported things went on in the rooms that were unexplainable. Items went missing, sounds were heard at night, and disturbing smells penetrated the walls.

Marie's uncle, John Franklin Jones, developed the water system and brought water to the Laurel Inn Hotel from the spring on Joe

White's Mountain next to the Inn. He also installed a water wheel that created hydroelectricity for the mills to be able to operate at night.

By 1905, many families gathered at Maple Grove Baptist Church and School, for basic learning, spiritual growth, and fellowship. The other church (a Methodist-Presbyterian) shared the building. The township had a company store, a speakeasy, and a train depot.

Due to a fire and a devastating flood in 1916, the town closed for the most part. Ghosts seemed to appear, but no one knows for sure. The town enjoyed a brief economic comeback. Mr. Mack Cook moved his family to the mill town so he could make a good living as a carpenter. The Civilian Conservation Corps arrived in 1933 with three hundred men to build the roads, trails, and buildings. This crew lived in tents and the Laurel Inn Hotel.

Mr. O. P. Lutz of Lenoir decided to buy the town and thousands of acres of the surrounding mountains. He had plans to rebuild and reopen the old mills to manufacture hosiery--even though he was warned against it by the local mountain people, who were familiar with the odd events that were blamed on the "ghosts."

Six machines were ordered from Germany, which came in boxes of thirty thousand pieces. Machinists put them together.

The plant had been operating for less than a week in August 1940, when ninety-four feet of rushing flood waters from Wilson Creek brought an end to the mill town. We remember families whose lives were lost during this disastrous time.

The mills and the railroad tracks and bridges were destroyed. The men of the CCC, whose camp was higher on the foothill, survived the flood, restored telephone, electricity, and repaired roads. They removed the railroad tracks, the story was told, to be used for the war effort.

The land as we now know it has rested peacefully for years. However, the concrete trestles, along with remains of the mills can still be seen. Hike the trails and experience the atmosphere of the area for yourself. Then kick back in your favorite chair, enjoy some tea, and imagine what it was like to be part of the adventure of Mortimer. Ask yourself: since we have explored the legend of the ghost town, the people who lived there, and the tales that were told, do ghosts still roam the creek and the remains of the mills? We may never know. You decide.

The Admiral's Flag
by
Stephen Downing

Summer, 1969. Corpus Christi, Texas, which is roughly halfway between the Western North Carolina Foothills (where I now reside) and Oregon State University. OSU, my alma mater, is nestled in the Willamette Valley between the Coast Range and the foothills of the Cascade Mountains.

I'm a Naval ROTC midshipman on summer training learning about Naval Aviation. I'm even getting a little 'stick time' in S-2 props and TF-9 jets. Yee Haw!!

It is late and dark. On this July night, man is about to take his first step onto the moon.

I am atop the Admiral's headquarters building with a couple other cohorts removing his flag. I shall not name names. (Not because of honor nor loyalty, but because I'm an old fart and can't remember…)

Seemed like a good idea at the time. Hey, I'm only 21 years old with a 'goldfish brain.' I didn't want the flag. I just liked the idea of seeing the flagpole barren the next morning when we marched to chow.

With everybody glued to their TV screens watching Neil Armstrong, we figured shore patrol (Naval military police) would also be indoors.

Good plan! We got the flag. No one got caught. Whoever kept the flag managed to get it mailed home or well-hidden from the contraband search the next day.

Couple weeks later at Naval Base Coronado, California, (amphibious training), we tried the same caper — minus the moon landing.

We got the flag, but also got caught climbing down the side of the building.

Shore patrol was pretty decent. The Admiral allowed as how he was pretty busy, he didn't think he should have to worry about dumbass middies trying to hoist his flag. Naturally, we agreed, pleaded for mercy, and were let go with a reprimand. (It's probably somewhere in my 'Permanent Record.')

And as for that naked flagpole at Corpus... Well, some sailor had run up the spare before daybreak!

DAMN!

Road Trippin'
Around the Foothills

Lost in a Foothill
by
Carol Starr

When my husband, Elliott, and I bought a brand-new house in a development, the yard had not even a blade of grass on it. We set about planting grass, flowers, and trees. I wanted a colorful tree near the driveway. A sorghum tree, *Nyssa sylvatica,* was what I was looking for.

I looked for local tree nurseries online. After visiting the first two on my list and not finding the tree, I headed for the last place. It was in a wooded area on a back road. The GPS took me there, but, alas, it turned out to be a wholesale nursery. Anyway, it did not have my tree.

Now it was getting late, so I set the GPS to take me the shortest route home. At first, the road was a usual two-lane road, winding through fields of corn and pastures. The GPS told me to turn right. This road was a bit smaller and headed into a hillier area.

"Turn right" the GPS, again, directed. Now the road had dwindled down to a small country lane and was not paved. It went by a group of small houses. One fellow, mowing his front yard, looked at my

Subaru curiously. I smiled confidently and continued according to instructions. The road was now down to a car and a half width. There was no way to turn around. By now, the road was only a path through the woods and one car wide. Then it began to wind up the side of a sizable foothill.

What happens if another car comes down the other way? I wondered. Finally, it reached the top of the tall hill and proceeded steeply down the other side. Luckily there had not been any traffic to deal with. Now I knew why that fellow had looked at me like that.

The GPS did take me home, and I still wonder where I had been that adventurous day.

P.S. I never did find a *Nyssa sylvatica.*

One Road Trip--With A Cherry On Top, Please
by
Stefanie Hutcheson

March is the kind of month that demands one takes a road trip. It's in the Geneva Convention! And who am I to argue with that legendary mandate?

Steve and I piled into our Subaru and headed west. We had a destination in mind and, after mapping it out and seeing there was a barbeque restaurant on the way, our decision was finalized. If there's anything we like more than road tripping, it's finding new places to eat!

From our home in Caldwell County, we drove about half an hour to Burke County. We knew that it was a cooler day but until we sat under the shelter of the Carolina Smoke Legendary Barbeque canopy with about a foot of sun shining on the both of us, we didn't realize how breezy it was. Didn't matter. The food was great and in huge proportions! I, of course, had the brisket; Steve the barbeque.

The next planned stop was to find the Lake James Dam. Somehow we missed our turn so we decided we'd go ahead and check out Sir James instead for a few minutes (plus we knew they had nice bathroom facilities--an important thing to know when one is out exploring). On the way there, though, we were enthralled with the Fonta Flora State Trail. There are many places to park, walk, and enjoy water activities here! Did I mention it was breezy? We enjoyed Mother Nature and her mesmerizing display of ripples and sunlight reflecting off the water. Fonta Flora is named after the local settlement of African-American sharecroppers, whose homes were flooded when the Catawba River was dammed to create Lake James.

Speaking of Mother Nature, we knew it was time to move on. A couple of cups of sweet tea will do that to travelers. Continuing on Hwy 126, we made our way to Lake James. After taking care of a couple of things, we took a few photos, admired more of God's handiwork, and took advantage of the wi-fi to find our original destination: Lake James Dam.

A year or two ago, we happened upon this road and I remember kicking myself. It is such a lovely drive! How could I have driven back and forth to Marion for nearly a year and not known of it? Located on Powerhouse Road, the lake is named for James Buchanan Duke, a tobacco tycoon and benefactor of Duke University. The lake has a surface elevation of twelve hundred feet and lies behind a series of four earthen dams. Unfortunately, there is not a  spot to pull over and admire this. However, the Good Lord was kind to us and only a few cars needed to pass us as we captured a few glimpses of His glory.

Surprisingly, after such a filling lunch, there was a sudden craving for what would just make this the perfect day: hot fudge cake! Giving Steve my best "pretty please," it wasn't hard to persuade him to make a slight detour after leaving McDowell County and make a pit stop at Abele's in Morganton. Telling me he wouldn't be able to eat any (mmn hmn), we were seated in a corner booth and soon served. Thankfully the waitress had dealt with fellas like him and brought us two spoons or poor Steve might have famished. Also, to end this jaunt on an even more positive note? She put three cherries on top. Who says you can't have it all?

Trip to the Cross
by
Thomas Blanton

Every now and then–sometimes every few months, or sometimes after a year or two–my wife Diane and I get the feeling we need to go see the Cross.

It's a hundred miles from our house to Lake Junaluska, NC but it is a beautiful drive. We feel we need to get away from our everyday lives and seek the peace we experience when we set foot on the grounds of the Lake Junaluska Assembly.

After a pleasant drive to the mountains, we arrive at the entrance gate, then follow the road across the dam, and up the hill.

We spend a night or two in one of the hotels on the grounds, enjoy a few hours rocking on a porch, browse the Cokesbury Bookstore, and often walk around the lake. When we are at Lake Junaluska we are revived.

During the days of our sojourn in the area, we walk around downtown Waynesville, have a meal or two at some of Waynesville's restaurants, eat a pastry at the Whitman Bakery, and browse the Mast General Store. We usually buy a few pieces of the candy from the barrels they have beside the checkouts, and then we're ready to come home.

We seldom leave the area without a stop at Barber Orchards Fruit Stand where we enjoy an apple fritter or glass of cider and buy a few apples for the trip home.

On the way home, we usually stop at the Farmer's Market in Asheville, and maybe have a meal at the Moose Café. Their half-runner beans are delicious with a country-style steak.

But the Cross is the main reason we go to Lake Junaluska. First erected in the 1920s, the metal cross, outlined in light bulbs, stands on a stone pedestal above the outdoor chapel.

Every trip, we feel drawn to stop and meditate at the foot of that cross. A restful peace comes over us when we walk around on the assembly grounds anyway, but standing at the foot of that cross is a soul-cleansing experience.

During World War II, when the whole country was blacked out at night and even the lights on Broadway went dim, the railroad engineers and conductors who drove the trains along the tracks that run by the lake begged the Assembly to keep the cross lights on. It was a beacon of hope in a dark time for them, and a symbol that the Lord was still in charge, despite the evil intentions of the Axis powers.

For Diane and me, this cross is a spot where we experience inspiration, peace, and renewal of our spirits. In fact, when this life is over, Diane and I both plan to have our ashes scattered on the hill below that Cross.

The Ultimate Road Trip
by
Gretchen Griffith

US Highway 64 is near and dear to my heart. I live within siren-wailing distance off that very road. For me, it's not just an ordinary, run-of-the-mill, get-me-to-work road, although for my entire career, it always was exactly that. Route 64 was also the start of all my road trips. When I drove east, staying on Hwy 64, I eventually ran into the Atlantic Ocean where the road terminates in the North Carolina Outer Banks. When I drove west on Hwy 64, I passed the schoolhouse I wrote about in one of my books. But if I were to drive farther west, farther, farther and farther, staying on Hwy 64 the whole distance, I'd arrive in Taos, New Mexico, six miles from my daughter's house.

One fall day, my husband and I started out on our ultimate road trip to visit our daughter. We began on the Carolina Foothills segment of Hwy 64, and then followed Interstate 40 through western North Carolina, Tennessee, Arkansas, Oklahoma, and Texas. Just after the state line in New Mexico, we took a side road across the mountains to Taos. Although the Interstate was efficient, it was full of potholes from the millions of heavy-duty caravans of semis traveling its backbone. This was a journey of two and a half days, not bad, except we were crammed in a pickup truck with plenty of room for odds and ends in the bed, including his golf clubs. With only two seats in the cab, the half-space was filled with overnight luggage, pillows, and the all-important food stash and ice cooler. We arrived drained of energy from hours of cramping our legs and pushing ourselves to make mileage goals.

We visited for a week and helped renovate the back deck of her house. From there I could sip tea and watch hot air balloons dotting the early morning horizon above the Rio Grande. In our leisure, we discussed an exciting possibility for our route home. Forget the interstate. We decided to drive home completely on US Highway 64

East. We plotted the route on a map, not hard to do. Drive six miles from her house, get on Hwy 64, follow the arrows, drive over a thousand miles, and get off a quarter mile from our house. No cheating. We would follow this road regardless, we pledged. Ha!

"Be sure to stop in Cimarron at the St. James Hotel," a friend told us over breakfast the morning of our departure and St. James it was – our first major find on our journey. We stopped in and walked through the lobby where once upon a time the likes of Buffalo Bill, Annie Oakley, Kit Carson, Jesse James, Wyatt Earp, and Billy the Kid had also stopped in and walked through the very same, unchanged lobby. Talk about feeling history!

Highway 64 took us all the way through the panhandle of Oklahoma, followed by the remainder of the state that makes up the pan to go with the handle. The sight out our back window showed an almost endless ribbon trailing us, and little, if any, traffic, a huge contrast to our

interstate travel coming west. We spent one night in Enid, Oklahoma, a real place to me now after years of filling the name in on crossword puzzles. We found an extinct volcano. We found salt flats. We found a distributor selling tornado shelters. We found Okies from Muskogee. We found Cherokee, Oklahoma and drove a few miles off route to the museum of the Western Cherokee Nation. Our eyes were opened seeing and hearing the Cherokee perspective beyond the North Carolina boundaries. We drove the backcountry through Arkansas on a route that appeared to us as quicker and shorter than the huge dip Interstate 40 takes to Little Rock.

We crossed the Mississippi on the Interstate 40 bridge, (no other choice) and picked up Hwy 64 again in Memphis, Tennessee. Off the beaten path, in the backwoods of southern Tennessee, we read Trail of Tears signs along the route of the highway as we followed it. I walked a few steps on the trail to take photographs thinking of those Cherokee who once were herded like sheep along the same route.

We crossed into North Carolina early on the final travel day and assumed we would be home in a few hours. Wrong.

Highway 64 goes through some of the most rugged land North Carolina has to offer. The road itself was bypassed by newer much smoother highways, but we stayed true to 64. When the sign said "No thru trucks" we should have realized what was in store, but we were determined to follow this route all the way, even if it meant cliffhangers. Cliffhangers we found.

Going off the beaten path meant no traffic jams, or so we thought. What we did find was a river-rafting traffic jam instead at the Oconee River.

We knew we were almost home when we wound our way down the mountain at Bat Cave and passed Lake Lure to drive along the Foothills of the Blue Ridge Mountains for the final hour.

Will we do it again?

No. Even though this highway is near and dear to my heart, and even though it was well worth the effort, we are done with US Highway 64. There are other backroads and by-ways waiting to be explored. Someday.

Road Trippin' Around the Foothills
by
Lucy Wilkes

Road trips around the Foothills are always adventures to be experienced. In Boone, Blowing Rock, and Valle Crucis there is something to do and to see amidst the beauty of it all.

My husband, Preston, and I started on an exploration of "where the road leads to" adventure one spring morning. We began in Lenoir following State Route 90 North. As we traveled, the scenery changed from houses to farms to trees along the road to thick woods, and then the road changed from pavement to gravel. We had traveled on gravel roads before on a shortcut, so we thought since it was shown on the map, through the mountains of Tennessee and North Carolina we would be safe. However, this road seemed different as we continued our trek.

Soon the road turned from gravel to dirt and I felt anxious. "Baby, can we turn around?"

"Awwwww, this is just a road, it comes out somewhere," was the answer.

I replied, "Hopefully we are not in someone's driveway."

Preston stopped when we approached a concrete bridge in front of us. A young man stood fishing from the side of the bridge as his hunting dog barked at our car.

Preston got out of the car and went to ask him where we were. I stayed in the car because of the barking dog and the stranger. I watched as they talked a bit and my husband rubbed the hound's head.

Upon arriving back at the car, Preston shared the news. "We are at the foot of Grandfather Mountain in the community called the Globe."

As we looked at each other, then the dirt road, the woods around us, and the darkness of the sky, we made the decision to turn around and go home. We had had enough of this adventure for now on the back roads of Caldwell County. More road trippin' adventures would have to wait for another time.

Road Trippin'
by
Michael (MJ) FitzGerald

It was a dark and rainy night as I trepidatiously entered the Pigeon River Gorge with a "reefer" (refrigerated trailer). I was going to plunge into a demanding stretch of road - one which challenges veteran drivers - as a 'newbie' solo driver hauling nearly 76,000 pounds over an unfamiliar, wet, and crowded road.

"What? Me worry?"

The Pigeon River Gorge is the narrowed, winding, twisting, undulating twenty miles of interstate at the far western end of I-40 in North Carolina. The Gorge's "Protected Area" extends eight-plus miles into Tennessee. Virtually the entire section in North Carolina is contained in the scenic Pisgah National Forest. Its curvy path runs generally north by northwest along the river, just east of the Cataloochee Divide marking the boundary between the "Old North" and the "Volunteer" States. Much of this descending, rising, curvy roadway has concrete barriers on both sides. These serve to protect from rocks falling off the canyon walls and also protect from oncoming vehicles on a road with no median. Additionally, the Gorge has many sections with little to no shoulder at all. Beyond the barrier, steep mountain walls alternate with steep drop-offs to the river. Not a place to daydream if you are the driver.

When road conditions are combined with darkness, wet and/or wintry weather, early and nighttime fog, and, most importantly, a continual flow of methodical or impatient drivers pushing forty-ton rigs on tight schedules with considerable variation not only in temperament but also experience, you have a recipe for earning your money. And you also have a recipe for earning considerably more difficulties than hard-earned money if you are not attentive to each and every passing rig.

Conditions being whatever they were, I needed to deliver my goods to Tennessee or Missouri (the memory is not perfect) on schedule and I-40's Pigeon River Gorge was the primary route to the destination. Having a few months of solo driving under my belt, I was neither sheepish nor cocky when viewing, before GPS days, the route on a

76

map. It was the only direct route to the regions of Tennessee I needed to traverse. I had been through the Gorge twice already, each time a new driver with an experienced trainer as co-driver in the passenger seat, one by day, the other by night.

Cautiously confident, then, might be an apt description for me, as I studied my route before leaving my loading point. Studying a map, however, is vastly different from rolling your rig into the Gorge for your first solo journey through it - in the midnight hours, in a sweeping rain, in a posse of truckers determined to get the Interstate reward of a rural straightaway waiting just beyond the Tennessee portion of the Gorge.

"It's just American business," I told myself as I noted the increasing westbound procession of trucks once I had cleared the late-night Asheville traffic. Then the approaching front's squalls began dousing the highway intermittently until it arrived with unremitting, lashing sheets of rain, swirling from new directions with each curve or change in terrain. And this was before arriving at the Gorge!

Recognizing this was not to be the calm route study I had imagined back in Charlotte, I girded my resolve to see it through. "Other truckers are here," I thought. "Surely I can keep pace through the turns and maintain my lane." And, with such a mindset newly formed, I entered the Gorge.

Well, I had barely put a mile under my wheels, and had nicely handled (I thought) a few of the Gorge's turns, when I came upon a 'prudent' methodical truck driver traveling at ten miles below the speed limit. "Nice," I thought, "I'll just cozy up behind him, and weave my way through" what was fast becoming an increasingly misted, drenched, and drenching stretch of road.

In less than two miles of this pull-in-your-horns travel mode, I was forced to jettison the idea altogether. Trucks were flying by us at the speed limit and higher, slapping my windshield with so much water the wipers were doing a joke of a job. What sealed the deal for me, the newbie solo driver, to commit to the passing lane for most of the remaining 25 miles of the Gorge was the second of two drivers high-tailing it in the slow lane who nearly smacked my trailer. They obviously thought - they certainly acted as though - all truckers were doing the speed limit or better, in both lanes, whatever the weather conditions. Blinking their lights while braking and downshifting, they allowed other speed limit trucks in the passing lane to glide past us, then quickly changed into the passing lane before other trucks gained on them. You could almost feel their curses as they went by.

Another word about the Gorge's curves and the passing lanes in wet, not to mention drenching, weather. Two things. The water on your windshield can, at times, virtually blind you to the road. Secondly, I quickly learned the differing effects of inside and outside curves when a truck passes. When, for instance, you are traveling west, the inside curves (toward the mountain in most instances) are *away* from the passing lane, while the outside curves (toward the river in most instances) are turning *toward* the passing lane. On the inside curve, your tractor's tires are, therefore, showering the passing truck. When you are being passed on the outside curve, however, look out! You are about to experience a tsunami on your windshield.

It did not take many trucks passing me on outside curves to convince me, thoroughly, that this was not the way I wanted to drive through the Gorge. Forget methodical, prudent, slow style. I was joining the pack. To do otherwise would mean continual passes of trucks doing the speed limit. And this meant substantially more high-risk moments where two trucks were side by side in a concrete barrier roadway negotiating inside or outside curves under soaking conditions.

Instinctively, some "new guy" mathematical probabilities portion of my brain locked in on the fact that staying in the slow lane would necessitate more of these side-by-side truck situations since most trucks were traveling at, or slightly above, the speed limits. Getting in the passing lane, despite my speed reluctance, meant fewer passes, and these would be made past slower, very cautious, or heavily loaded trucks. Further, these truck passes could be made at my pace. I could choose whether the higher risk side-by-side moments occurred on an inside or an outside curve.

With an "If you can't beat 'em, join 'em" attitude, then, I committed to the passing lane by the fourth mile, on that rainy night through the Gorge. It poured rain all the way. My knuckles were white after gripping my steering wheel for the next twenty-five miles. My palms sweated like open faucets while I weaved back and forth through those unrelenting curves, and slower trucks.

By mile three, behind the slower truck, I realized there was no turning back. If I was to deliver my load, I must continue, and, if I was to continue, I had better do it in the safest manner possible. The safest

78

manner meant taking the risk with the haulers in the fast lane. This risk meant not only our rainy concrete bordered lanes, our speeds, the onset and direction of the next curve, and the nearby four-wheelers thinking it's fun to dodge speeding rigs on a rainy night, but my resolve to *survive* my next pass and deliver my load on time. It *always* feels good to "bump the (loading) dock," but it felt particularly good to bump this load the next day.

By day, the Pigeon River Gorge has breathtaking scenery. There are sheer canyon walls, parallel and perpendicular, long sightlines of the tumbling Pigeon River, stark and stunning seasonal variations, ridgelines, peaks, and cascades.

I always seek to see it in these visible hours. When doing so, though, I never fail to reflect on my first solo truck trip through the Gorge, hammer down, driving rain, hub to hub, between concrete barriers, maintaining our lanes, and navigating our way through the next turn.

Journey to Shiloh
by
Kathy Lyday

It was past time for a road trip. It only took an hour from Hickory driving on I-40 East, then I-77 North, finally taking exit 65 to Union Grove on Hwy 901. Lush farmland lined the curvy Memorial Highway. Guinea hens crossed the road, expecting cars to wait for them. When I reached my destination--Shiloh General Store in Hamptonville, North Carolina--I was filled with anticipation, since I had visited before.

Shoppers step up to the front porch which is lined with tall chairs, each having a footrest. There is also a ramp for those who prefer that option. Not knowing where to start, I decided to take a stroll around the perimeter. When I opened the door, I was immediately wreathed in the aroma of fresh bread baking. Then I began to walk around struck by sensory overload. Color swirled around me and it took a few moments to focus my eyes.

I had to start somewhere so I went over to the pickles. They have pickled everything that you can think of--even cloves of garlic. Over one shelf there was a sign that said, "Be strong and courageous." I walked on and perused the kaleidoscope of jellies and jams, spices, coffees, cappuccinos, teas, baking supplies, bulk grains, and cooking utensils. I had never before seen Christmas or Banana Split Jam. The dairy case, supplied by a nearby creamery, holds assorted cheeses, yogurts, and rolls of butter. I smelled fresh peanuts being ground into peanut butter and I  picked up a round of pepper jack cheese and some yogurt. The frozen food available includes Moravian chicken pies, vegetables, bacon, sausage, grass-fed beef, and much more... I walked on, overwhelmed by the bounty and variety. The store sells colorful quilts, furniture, and even dog houses! Finally, I reached my favorite place-the deli/bakery.

Shirley and Richard Graeber, owners of the Shiloh General Store, have baked their own bread for years. Sourdough, wheat, multigrain, sundried tomato and rye breads are sold in unsliced loaves. Day-old bread is used for made-to-order deli sandwiches. Customers fill out order slips with their name and sandwich choices and a smiling Amish girl in a long dress, with a cap and apron, makes the sandwich and places it on the counter with the order slip. The sandwich bread is sliced thickly--like Texas toast. A wide selection of meats and cheeses is available and customers can add a variety of relishes and other condiments for the "fully involved" sandwich.

On Saturday mornings, freshly made donuts are available until they sell out. The cinnamon rolls are large and fragrant; you can smell them as you stand beside the shelf. I selected a fried peach pie from the rack and it was still warm from the oven. There were so many individual and full-size pies of varying flavors--coconut, chocolate, cherry, banana cream, lemon, pecan, raspberry, and more. Imagine any kind or color of popcorn and they had it.

The candy and snack aisle would tempt anyone with its fanfare of rainbow colors and flavors. I noticed an old-fashioned bridge mix, a variety of chocolate-covered nuts, that my mother would have liked. She used to serve that to her monthly bridge club. I passed that up and walked past the herbal remedies section. I noticed a Super Tonic. The instructions were to take one tablespoon daily and if you were sick to take one tablespoon hourly.

Circling back to the deli, I saw my order slip on top of my sandwich, a chicken salad with sweet relish. I took that and my other selections up to the pleasant young Amish man at the cash register dressed in high collared short-sleeved blue shirt, suspenders and gray pants. I had fleeting thoughts of adding other items but then resisted temptation.

I ventured out to the porch and selected a tall chair. I savored the fresh air and perfect sandwich and reflected on the experience with appreciation. What a lovely respite! As I drove away, I was already planning a return trip.

Musicians, Artists, and Other Beautiful Foothillers of the Community

"Red Tree" Acrylic Painting, 12x12, by Linda LaRose

Heroes Haikus
by
Stephen Downing

HEROES

Good guys wear a mask
behind the counter, behind
the takeout window

GROCERIES

Food Lion cashier
working today, every day
thank you and stay safe

FUMIYOSHI

My hero takes cash,
my order, gives correct change,
hibachi chicken

CVS

Pharmacist says hi
six nine, nineteen forty-nine
prescription ready

Heart and Soul of the Foothills
by
Lucy Wilkes

Let's start our story with authors. What do we really know about authors? They are creative word weavers who are given to the imagination of the soul. Persons who give existence to words while captivating readers and pulling them into places they have never been before. Influencers who spark memories of the past hidden in the recesses of the mind all the while making new paths to explore.

One of the greatest authors I've read is C.S. Lewis, creator of *The Chronicles of Narnia, The Space Trilogy,* and *Mere Christianity,* among other works. His writings inspire the reader to come on an adventure of whimsical travels to other worlds. Lewis's books have embedded in them a spiritual undertone with a sense of what moral behavior is. Even in dangerous situations, the goodness and kindness of others win favor.

For children and adults alike, the series *Mandie,* by Lois Gladys Leppard, is an easy read. Encountering adventures and solving mysteries with friends gives the reader a taste of childhood that may have been yearned for while growing up. These writings take place in North Carolina where Lois grew up.

Closer to home in the Foothills we have an array of local authors who have written books to satisfy every intrepid spirit. Tales of hometowns, road trips, adventures, faith, and even memories left behind. Some books have a bit of local history, folklore, and poetry to muse upon. A creative literary work can be captured by anyone who desires to obtain a treasure or two.

Is there an author inside waiting to burst forth? Think about it. The imagination is an expression of a ready writer. Whether putting down thoughts in a diary, stories in a journal, or even posting dreams of the past night's sleep, all come from the author within.

Every good and perfect gift is from above, and comes down from the Father of lights with whom there is no variableness, neither shadow of turning. James 1:17 (NKJV)

84

Imagine words set to musical notes. What do you hear? Poems, stories, love ballads, or the rhythm of your own heart? Is this where the magic begins? In our heart lies a memory of each and every thing we have heard, felt, seen, or fancied. Musicians are creators who know words are powerful and reach into places we have forgotten.

As the tune plays in your mind, does your toe want to tap as the body desires to sway or does the soul wish to remember how to play? Yes is the answer. Music is the universal language between body, soul, and spirit. Remember how the songs *Amazing Grace, How Great Thou Art, and I Can Only Imagine* stirred our hearts with respect to our Creator? Oh yes, music can be part of our being. Remember the 50s, 60s, and 70s music? *Jailhouse Rock, The Monster Mash, Raindrops Keep Falling On My Head,* and many more. Yes, music is part of our being.

Here in the Foothills, Doc Watson was a singer of bluegrass, folk, and gospel music. Whenever he got a chance, he would sit down and strum out tunes. A barber shop in Drexel had a back room, not for poker, but for Doc and others that brought their instruments to play. On Saturday, getting a haircut and listening to live music was something to look forward to. Doc was a pillar in our community, for sure.

One time when we were camping, my husband played his guitar with his brother who played his saxophone in the evening. People gathered to listen. We were amazed how much pleasure the music gave to the audience. Of course the brothers enjoyed themselves also.

A baby can fall asleep as a lullaby is sung. The soul becomes peaceful when soft rain and flutes are heard. Yes, music has an effect on our hearts. When David the shepherd boy played his stringed instrument, Saul (the king of Israel) became calm and restful. Music is a gift to us to enjoy.

Words are powerful with or without music. Languages that are spoken, read, or sung, influence our heart and soul in some way. As the Bible says, *How delightful is a timely word.* Next time you read a book, listen to music, or hear someone speak, think about what gift lies inside waiting to be expressed.

A Not So Famous Guy
by
Michael (MJ) FitzGerald

So there's this guy who sits at the end of the bar in our local pub-restaurant and almost daily orders a large garden salad. He covers it with pepper, lots of pepper - and I mean really lots of pepper. That kinda guy. Unusual.

"So what?" you may think. The Foothills are crowded with all kinds of unusual guys.

Yeah, all kinds of unusual guys, but have they donated the initializing endowment for their town's Greenway without wanting recognition? Granted, not everyone has a Greenway to their credit, anonymous or otherwise. Nor have they spent decades at Harvard University, including studying at, at least, four other universities. Not likely to be credentials shared with many other residents of the Foothills.

This guy has individually taken on at least two large banks in years-long legal battles, potentially yielding significant settlements. Such settlements, in the likely range of billions of dollars nationally, are destined to acquire additional public use lands for the enjoyment of the states' citizens.

Again, these lawsuits seek to hold accountable the banks which generated thousands of fraudulent checking and savings accounts and false loans, ruining individuals' credit ratings in the process. By deceptively directing funds to justify executive and employee bonuses, these banks and their distorted banking policies violated the trust of their depositors rather than stimulating economic growth through legal, honest loans.

The citizens' financial laws have been ignored. Class action lawyers and arbitrators (in Delaware in particular) have "side-stepped" past the legal, prescribed penalties for financial fraud by seeking "class action" settlements in favor of big banks. These settlements have not imposed the prescribed penalties for each individual instance of fraud. But there's an unusual salad guy (he studied law at both Harvard and

Georgetown) who is methodically working his way through the courts (State and Federal) in an attempt to hold these banks accountable.

Yes, this guy's unusual - and interesting, and pedigreed, and afflicted. His mobility-limiting disease (MS) does not prevent a weekly hike up Hibriten Mountain with his dog. "The alternative of mobility is a compelling incentive to keep walking," he explains with a shrug of his shoulders, "as are my dog's howls of delight as we approach Hibriten's parking lot." Though not a doctor, he comes from a line of physicians stretching past the Civil War and Sherman's siege of Atlanta, with doctors on both sides of the family.

Returning to his Foothills in mid-life, having come home (from Harvard) to care for his cancer-stricken mother, he has again settled here, staying after her death. Her name is prominently displayed on the Greenway, on signs made out of cedar, her favorite perfume scent. Now he peppers his salad, reads the books he has always intended to read, and prepares legal briefs for his seemingly never-ending actions against billion-dollar banks. He punctuates these activities by working part-time with the disabled and homebound.

Yep, the Foothills have plenty of unusual folks, and our salad guy, in many ways, is just another not-so-famous character. If you have a hankering, though, for a conversation on the arts, the sciences (pick them, he has degrees in at least two), medicine, the law, sports (tennis and hiking in particular), travel (he has hiked Europe from the Arctic Circle to the Mediterranean), or a local charity, he's your guy.

The 1841 Cafe in downtown Lenoir, almost any night. Look for the salad covered with pepper.

Forrest ("Smoky") Burgess
by
Thomas Blanton

Forrest Burgess, known as "Smoky," is one of the greatest sports stars to come out of the Foothills of North Carolina. One day as Dizzy Dean was broadcasting a game involving the Chicago White Sox, he commented, "Who's that great group of people walking up to the plate? Oh, it's Smoky Burgess." This incident was toward the end of his career when age had put some extra pounds on him. Still, he went down in history as having the most career pinch hits (145) of any baseball player in the major leagues.

Smoky was born in Caroleen, NC, in 1927, and started his baseball career in 1944. From 1949 on, he played in the major leagues, first with the Chicago Cubs, then with the Philadelphia Phillies, the Cincinnati Reds, the Pittsburgh Pirates, and finished his playing days with the Chicago White Sox.

He played in five All-Star games during his career, and had a lifetime batting average of .295, with 126 home runs, 673 RBI, and a .362 on-base percentage.

As catcher for the Pirates, Smoky led his team to a World Series championship in 1960. His batting average in that season was .333. In 1963, he was traded to the Chicago White Sox where he finished his career as a pinch hitter. In his first appearance at the plate, Smoky hit a game-tying home run against the Detroit Tigers. In 1966, he set a major league record for the most games played by a non-pitcher without scoring a run: 79 games.

At the age of forty, Smoky retired from playing and returned to Rutherford County, to his home in Forest City. He did some scouting for the Atlanta Braves and worked as the batting coach for the minor-league Pulaski Braves. He also lent his name to a fitness center run by a local chiropractor in Forest City, as well as being part owner of an Esso service station in town.

Smoky was inducted into the Cincinnati Reds Hall of Fame in 1975 and into the North Carolina Sports Hall of Fame in 1978. But for all his talent, he never let his fame go to his head. He died in 1991 at the age of sixty-four, a humble son of the Foothills to the end.

Someone to Remember
by
Kathy Lyday

When she hugged you, she hugged harder than a woman usually would, as if she wanted to absorb something from deep inside you. Her welcoming smile and gentle nature made me feel like the earth revolved around me. The combined aroma of green beans cooking in an iron pot and Maxwell House coffee hit me when I walked in her house. I remember her twinkling blue eyes, her husky voice, and her love of snuff. I wish she had had an easier life.

Born and raised on a farm, she ended up always living on one. She ran away from home and got married at sixteen. They had a baby boy. Unfortunately, six months later, her husband was killed, falling off the back of a pickup truck as it made a turn. She found work in a textile factory to support herself and the baby.

Later she married a chicken farmer and had two more sons. One of the sons developed a brain tumor and passed away at age eleven. There were fewer treatments back then. The other son developed a drug habit which led to incarceration. The day after he swore to get clean, he died from an overdose in prison. Unable to manage alcohol, the remaining son from her first marriage shot himself in a horse trailer, leaving a wife and two daughters.

One by one, from the youngest to the oldest, the children were gone.

The shape of her family changed radically, but she did not – except for taking up a new hobby: crocheting. On the rare occasions that she sat down, she picked up her yarn. She made afghans for everyone – those multi-colored squares that were all of the rage in the seventies. Mine was orange and green with some brown in it – a graduation gift. I did not realize until much later that the repetitive hand movements of crocheting and the act of holding the hands in front of the body create a protective bubble of personal space and comfort, while also releasing serotonin. That is one way that she chose to manage her pain – crafting something that would bring comfort to others. Many might have broken, but I barely saw her bend.

A lifelong Baptist, she was known in the community for her sweet nature, her work ethic, and her banana pudding. Her husband was overly domineering, but she never complained. Only her slumped shoulders divulged the secret that she was plodding down a difficult road. Psychologists today would question the way that she handled her grief.

I believe she gave it to God.

When I think of an extraordinary person, she is who comes to mind. She was not famous, not an artist, nor a musician, but an ordinary woman living with formidable loss and an iron faith in God, equipping her to triumph over multiple tragedies. I have never met a more genuine person with greater resilience. Her story deserved to be told.

Her name was Willie and she was my aunt.

Pillar Talk
by
Stefanie Hutcheson

Many folks are familiar with the King James Bible verse from John 1:46 that states: *And Nathanael said unto him, Can there any good thing come out of Nazareth? Philip saith unto him, Come and see.* It was said mockingly by Nathanael as Philip pondered Jesus. History has gone on to prove that yes, indeed, Virginia: something most excellent came from Nazareth!

When considering the Foothills of North Carolina, several folks come to mind that have put our region on the map. I could do some name-dropping and list a few musicians, athletes, congressmen and women, authors, inventors, and the like. However, instead, I choose to tell of some lesser-known pillars of the community. Lesser-known but in all likelihood more beloved by those whose lives have been touched because these souls' impact struck us on a more personal level. Personal as meaning a one-on-one relationship versus the casual in-passing sort that many use to somehow try to make ourselves look more exciting because we once had our picture made with rising country music star Alex Key, have a baseball signed by Madison Bumgarner, or saw Junior Johnson at the track in Wilkesboro as he won one of his many races.

But what about those other heroes? You know: the ones who don't wear capes--although they may often be found in uniforms. Law enforcement, rescue personnel, auto mechanics, and fast-food workers.

Fast-food workers are heroes? Puh-lease.

Indeed, fast-food workers. Have you ever tried getting to your destination and driven along Hwy 321? Chances are good that if you have, you've had to either wait until the traffic thinned or divert to the other lane so that you wouldn't get caught in the Bojangle's rush. Don't know what it is about those biscuits, but I daresay that hundreds of folks each day would be a bit miffy if their day didn't begin with one.

Does that make restaurant workers heroic? You tell me. Have you ever tried to feed your family and didn't have food in the house? The kids are squalling--starving in truth were you to ask them--and you knew if you could just get something in their sweet little bellies they would be all right. On your way to school, there were those golden arches, or the always welcome "Hot Doughnuts Now" inviting you to come and be the best mom ever. Mmn hmn. Thought so. I'll bet as the kiddos licked that last bit of icing from their elbow (we don't even ask anymore how they managed to get it there) on the way to class one of their friends inwardly groaned because their mom wasn't that cool, made them eat cereal for breakfast, and how they wished your parent was theirs instead. Thanks to these diligent workers, mom is able to save the day.

On a more serious level, what about those with the white coats? Yes, the hospital and doctor staff, surely, but I'm also thinking about your pharmacist. How many times has s/he explained to you that this drug interacts in such and such a way, to not eat a certain food with this one so that you won't be spending your night on the porcelain throne, or recommended exactly what was needed to combat that sickness that wasn't quite serious enough to warrant an urgent care visit?

Each day we are confronted with unsung pillars of our community. They look normal on the outside but what they do for us often saves the day. Vickie at the Sawmills Cafe tells you she's been praying for you over that thing you confided in her the week before and gives you a hug before you leave. Mike at the public library sees you coming and has your books and movies ready. Chad at the Cajah Mtn. Lube changes your oil and checks your fluids, reminding you those tires might need some air. The gal at Tim's Citgo sees you coming and automatically gets your roll of smokeless tobacco before you even have to ask. Sheila, Rachel, and Jill at Shields Hardware wait on you with a smile and inside info for that item you called about. And one of my favorites: on Wednesdays when I go to Donna's Cafe in Hudson, my tea and dumplins don't even have to be ordered. The gals just nod and bring them to me.

Sawyer fills the sanctuary with peaceful and cheerful tunes to set the tone before the service, sees you come in, and finds a way to slip your favorite hymn in because it's your special day. Erin at TCBY always gives you your treat with a smile and a question about how your family is doing. Danny Starnes rarely turns down a customer in need of electrical help--even at those odd hours or weird places that need an outlet put in. Kristi at the vision center makes sure those glasses are exactly the most flattering and functional pair you need.

93

The folks in our communities are just regular Joes and Janes. They do their jobs and collect their paychecks, the same as the rest of us. Right?

Unh-unh. They aren't the same and they aren't common. Used to be, but now? Now one has to look far and wide to find these heroes who help us with our basic needs, treat us as friends, and send us on our way with a genuine and sincere "have a nice day." Because of them, many of us do.

Pillars of the community. Thanks to them, we all can sleep better at night. Mike Lindell would be so proud.

Five Haiku
by
Carol Starr

Dependable

Fail-safe pharmacist
greets me by name and a smile
here's your insulin

Secret?

My sister tells me
I know your dirty secret
what? your microwave

Remembrance

November 11th
red poppies pinned on my dress
tribute...just a dime

Good Deeds

Three baby robins
one tiny possum I saved
from my curious dog

Oops

Nice fat blueberries
enough for a pie...I trip...
they roll down the hill

From Flanders Field to the Carolina Foothills
by
Gretchen Griffith

There's a heart-rending poem by Canadian John McCrae that honors fallen soldiers of a 1915 World War I battle in Belgium. I read it at least once a year, on Veteran's Day. As a physician on the front lines, McCrae witnessed carnage and bloodshed beyond description, yet he used the beauty of flowers in a place called Flanders to remind the world that those killed did exist.

This war continued and the Germans intensified their bombardments on northern France, not all that far away from the battlefield where McCrae set the poem. The American forces were on the ground and were the recipients of this constant barrage. In the midst of the fury was a unit once known as the Hickory Company of the National Guards, 105th Engineers, 30th Division. One of those wounded by bombs dropped from the German planes on July 17, 1918, was twenty-seven-year-old Private Albert Tuttle Corpening from the

small community of Gamewell in Caldwell County. He was taken to a hospital behind the lines where he died the following day and was buried in wartime haste at the American cemetery in France. His brother Wilfong Corpening was serving in the same unit and sent a letter to notify their parents, Albert and Eola Corpening. A memorial service was held in Lenoir at the First Methodist Church to honor his memory.

His body was disinterred and returned to Lenoir in January, 1921, where he was laid to final rest at the cemetery of his home church, Littlejohn Methodist. A memorial service was held at that time and was attended by many veterans not only of World War I, but also of the Civil War and the Spanish American War. They did not know Corpening but came to honor him.

Enthusiasm for honoring the war dead and caring for those who survived spread throughout the region and led to a reorganization of the Caldwell Post of the American Legion. At an August 1921 meeting, the group elected a slate of officers to be led by Post Commander F.D.

Grist. By unanimous vote the name of the post was to honor the first Caldwell County soldier to give his life in World War I, therefore it became the Albert Corpening Post.

The community held a huge Armistice Day celebration under the direction of the legion post on Friday, November 11, 1921. This included a grand veterans' parade, "moving pictures" of actual war scenes in Europe, and speeches from visiting dignitaries and members of the Albert Corpening Post. Dinner on the grounds of Davenport College was prepared by women's clubs from Caldwell County and followed by a football game between rivals Lenoir and Wilkesboro High Schools. The day ended with various old-time contests including sack races and greased pole climbing, and culminated with a street dance and promenade on the pavement. Poppies made by war orphans were sold.

Within a month after this massive celebration, the American Legion Post found themselves facing a necessary correction. In selecting the name of the post, they originally set out to honor the first Caldwell County soldier killed in the war. Upon further discovery, they became aware of two men, Private Charles Dysart and Corporal Jean Kendall who were killed in action in France on June 21, 1918, nearly a month before Corpening's death. The legion members voted to change the name to the more accurate Dysart-Kendall Post.

Wearing a poppy gives me an opportunity to honor those who have given their lives in battle. I am free to write these words in part because of their ultimate sacrifice. One of those soldiers who should never be forgotten is a man from the Foothills of North Carolina, Albert Tuttle Corpening.

Poems, Prayers, and Promises

To My New Mother-In-Law
by
Kathy Lyday

Now that I've wed your youngest precious son
I'll dedicate my life to serving him
I vow to clean and scrub; I'll make it fun
I'll dote upon his every little whim
I will prepare tasty foods that he likes
And always be tidy with dishes
I'll gently suggest that he ride his bike
And accompany him if he wishes
But if you think you can ever tell me
The way in which I should manage my house
You will indeed see, that I will not be
A woman faintly resembling a mouse
So, know right now on this glorious day
If I were you, I would watch what I say

Poems and Prayers
by
Lucy Wilkes

My Dear Friend

God sent me a friend
One of great esteem
An ear to lend
Together we're a team
A lot in common do we have
Love of God, art, music
Her words are like a salve

She speaks with authority
But not too quick

Talented is she as she paints with ease
Master of the brushes, paper, paint, and more
Watercolors, acrylics, and oils all of these
Become willing subjects to adore

Bless her Lord
With all Your heavenly Love
And the mysteries You can afford
Genuinely sent from above

Haiku Poems

Blooming daylilies
How brilliant you are to see
Shut out the darkness
****

To teach is to touch
Brilliant minds are opened up
A life forever
****

What shall we do now
Think, explore, research, type, write
Just one more you see
****

Earth, fire, sky, sea
All the created order
For all to behold
****

What is for supper
Chili on the stove you know
Smell the air yum yum
****

Sometimes

Sometimes… You call me
In the cool of the eve
Often I hear Your voice
And come running by choice

Sometimes… when things go astray
Upward my glance is drawn
To search for Your face
My heart and thoughts race

Sometimes… to Your word I run
Complete in You, we are one
Your word I absorb as I desire
The love I sense, it sparks a fire

Sometimes… alone I sit and meditate
Thinking, enjoying, and learning to appreciate
The loving things You do and say
To bring me along on life's way

Sometimes… I whisper Your name
From the first time, I've never been the same
It is the power of heaven and earth
Through it I received a second birth

Sometimes… in Your grace I stand in awe
Holy, righteous, and without flaw
How could I ever be like You?
How could we be one and not two?

Sometimes… these things are too rich for me
Only in the Spirit can I see
How much You love Your bride to be
For You gave Your life on a tree

Sometimes… when my glance is below
Your voice calls, come, to You I'll show
How to glide high and free
Up here with Father and Me

Sometimes… Oh, my Lord
Your abundant love makes my heart soar
Your fragrance engulfs my being
A sacrifice of heart I bring

Sometimes… Jesus can't You see
The broken alabaster box of oil set free
To hear Your heart, obey Your voice
On bended knee I made my choice

Prayers

Dear Lord, I come to You, it is the only thing I know to do.

With my heart breaks, problems, and concerns, let me leave them here with You. Your word tells me that You care about everything that is important to me.

So here I am asking for Your to help again. Your word says to ask and it will be given, knock and it will be opened, seek and you will find, so I'm asking and receiving the answers by faith. Thank You, Father God. Amen.

Excuses
by
Stefanie Hutcheson

I wanted to write a song
But felt like they'd all been sung

I wanted to write a poem
But truly there is nothing new under the sun

I wanted to write a prayer
But was too far from the altar

I wanted to write a promise
But was afraid it wouldn't be kept

I wanted to write a letter
But the story was too long

I wanted to write an ode
But I have too many Billy Joes

I wanted to write an epistle
But my wisdom wasn't complete

I wanted to write an apology
But found I wasn't really sorry

I wanted to write a mystery
But my detective skills were lacking

I wanted to write a how-to
But realized I was clueless

I wanted to write a children's story
But wasn't able to use my best examples

I wanted to write an essay
But kept getting off topic

I wanted to write a tale
But found I was too short

I wanted to write an anthem
But the cause kept changing

I wanted to write an argument
But found out I couldn't win

I wanted to write a book
And there I found myself

According to Jesus' Enemies
by
Thomas Blanton

Herod said, "Show me where he is."
Lord, let us seek You and let us find You in our hearts.

The Pharisees said, "He eats with sinners."
Come dine with us, Lord, and cleanse us from our sins.

The Herodians said, "You show no deference."
Thank You, Lord, for treating us all as equals, no matter how You created us to be.

Pilate asked, "Are you the King of the Jews?"
Reign in our world, O King of the Universe, and rule over all our hearts.

Caiaphas said, "It is better for one man to die for the sake of the nation."
Thank You, Lord Jesus, for giving up Your life to save our nation and our world.

The priests said, "He saved others; he cannot save himself."
Thank You, Lord, that You did not save Yourself and leave us to die in our sins.

The Centurion said, "Surely this was the son of God."
Thank You, God, for sending us Your Son to save us.

The demons asked, "What have you to do with us, Son of God?"
Yes, Lord, what do You have for us to do in Your Kingdom?

Five Questions
by
Carol Starr

Who?

Children in a room
just learning some ABCs
threaten nobody

What?

See the atmosphere
in today's news...violence
comes from everywhere

When?

Peaceful yesterdays
even before we knew--gone
yes, gone, with the wind

Where?

Now we do not know
what evil will show its face
in our neighborhood

Why?

People do not need
assault guns in the forest
just to kill a deer

Waver
by
Michael (MJ) FitzGerald

To tarry or to go
To be or not to be a different you;
To see the light in a child's eye
    glow
Or to marvel at the dusk of a desert
    hue;

The functional exchange of coin for
    goods
Where pause for the other is a
    different you;
Linger by the summer woods
Or to the next task swiftly do?

Alone or another
Sight to see;
The babe at the mother,
Crooning glee.

The dawn is gray before the rise-
Be it crest/ridge, surf, or city -
Light's gathering day neither old nor wise,
Glint to the wave, while we waver
    Pretty

Recipes

Tom's Famous Soup
by
Thomas Blanton

When I became single again, I started eating healthier than before. I was advised to save my leftover vegetables to use in soup, so I devised this recipe to follow that advice. Most of the time, though, when I make it I seldom have any leftovers. Usually, it is all new ingredients. Still, it has gotten rave reviews whenever I've served it.

INGREDIENTS
–The smallest package of stew beef the supermarket has (a pound or less)
–A couple of peeled medium potatoes (or a few redskins, new potatoes, or a 12-oz. can of potatoes)
–A couple of medium carrots (or several baby carrots)
–A medium onion
–A 12-oz. can of tomatoes
–A package of frozen vegetables (or a 12-oz. can of Veg-All)
–One bay leaf
–Salt and pepper to taste
–Optional: any leftover frozen beans, peas, etc. you may choose to add

Trim the fat off the meat, cut it into bite-sized pieces, and drop it into a 4-quart pot. Cover with water and place on the burner. Turn it to HIGH.
Cut the potatoes, carrots, and the onions into bite-sized pieces and drop them into the pot.
Open the can of tomatoes and dump them into the pot.
Add the frozen vegetables, the bay leaf, and the salt and pepper.
Stir.
When the water comes to a boil, lower the heat and cook for at least 45 minutes, stirring occasionally.

Serves 6-8.

Mom's Shortbread Cookies
by
Carol Starr

Ingredients:

1 cup salted butter
½ cup superfine sugar
2 ½ cups cake flour
Pinch of salt

Cream butter. Add sugar. Add flour and salt.

Divide into 3 rolls.

Wrap each roll in wax paper and square off the edges.

Chill overnight in refrigerator.

Slice 1/4" thick.

Bake on a parchment-lined cookie sheet at 375° F for approximately 8-1/2 minutes or until edges just start to brown. (You have to check on them at about 8 minutes.)

Cool for 10 minutes, remove from the pan, and put on a rack to finish cooling.

Notes:

This is a simple recipe, with three basic ingredients, easy to make, and quite yummy!
You can freeze the dough and thaw it in the refrigerator, then bake it, if you wish to make it at a later date.

Nutrition information:
Each recipe = 3155 calories and 338 carbohydrates
1 cookie = 130 calories and 14 carbs

111

Recipes
by
Lucy Wilkes

My favorite recipes are from those who are good cooks, which I am not. A dear friend of mine and I were working on baking cookies for Christmas when she asked me to roll out wedding cookies. We always made cookies as a customer appreciation gift for our faithful clients. Of course, I said yes, not knowing how sticky the dough was. She didn't realize I could not stand my hands to become covered with stuff.

After a few rolls with my hands, I quit and asked if I could help in some other way because I had to wash my hands. After explaining to her about the way I felt about sticky stuff on my hands, she gave me the task of cutting up fruit. *Oh good*, I thought, *this job would not cause my hands to feel dirty.* Little did I know the fruit she had was candied cherries, pineapple, raisins, and nuts. Being too embarrassed to ask to change tasks again, I endured and cut up all the ingredients then washed my hands. We finished baking cookies.

Now when I enjoy the fruitcake cookies from her recipe, a remembrance of our baking day floods my mind again, and a smile crosses my face.

Lucy's Fruitcake Cookies

1 lb. candied cherries	1 tsp. vanilla
1 lb. candied pineapples	1 tbs. lemon flavoring
1 lb. white raisins	3 c. flour
4 c. chopped nuts	1 tsp. salt
½ c. flour (all-purpose)	1 tsp. cinnamon
1 ½ c. sugar	1 tsp. baking soda
1 c. butter salted or unsalted (2 sticks)	
⅓ c. milk	2 eggs

Dredge cherries, pineapples, raisins, and nuts in ½ cup flour. Cream together sugar and butter. Add eggs one at a time. Add flavorings. Sift flour, salt, and soda together. Add the mixture with milk and combine well. Add floured fruit. Spoon onto a greased cookie sheet. Bake at 325° for 15 minutes. Yields about 200 cookies. Enjoy!

No-Apple Apple Zucchini Pie

My son-in-law hates the veggie zucchini. And what does that have to do with apple pie, you may ask? Well, the story goes like this. You guessed it. Was there a way to make an apple pie with zucchini that he could not tell what it was made of? The answer is yes. Amazingly, it is true.

Use a large zucchini
Peel and cut in quarters lengthwise
Remove seeds
Cut crosswise into smaller pieces
Cook and drain, about 4 cups
Set aside.

Toss together:
2 Tbsp. lemon juice
Dash of salt

Mix in a bowl:
1 ¼ c. sugar
1 ½ tsp. cinnamon
1 ½ tsp. cream of tartar
Dash of nutmeg
3 Tbsp. flour (all-purpose)

Add zucchini and mix well. It will be runny but that is okay.

Put in a 9-inch deep-dish crust following the directions on the package. Dot with butter (salted or unsalted).
Add top crust and place pie on cookie sheet.
Bake @ 400° for 40 minutes or until brown on top.
Don't tell them that it is not apples until everyone is finished eating and watch their faces.
Surprise! Enjoy the no-apple apple zucchini pie.

Pimento Cheese
by
Kathy Lyday

3 ounces cream cheese
¼ teaspoon salt
¼ teaspoon garlic powder
¼ teaspoon black pepper
½ cup mayonnaise
1 cup grated pepper jack cheese
1 cup grated sharp cheddar cheese
1 teaspoon grated onion
1-2 teaspoons chopped pimentos

Beat cream cheese with an electric mixer until light and fluffy. Add other ingredients. Chill. Serve cold with crackers or stuff celery with it. Serve hot as grilled pimento cheese sandwiches.
The pepper jack can be swapped for something else; smoked gouda is good in place of it.

Sam's Blackberry Cream Pie, Chilled
by
Michael (MJ) FitzGerald

Quick and easy "go-to" recipe for a "sure-fire" crowd pleaser after a busy day of skiing, hiking, shopping, etc. and you are plain too tired to bake a pie. Will please as surely as a chiffon or meringue delivery to the table. Sam's Mom has served this dessert for years as an accent for a special family meal, and Sam has happily saved it for her table.

Ingredients:
- 1 Graham Cracker Pie Crust
- 1 standard Cool Whip tub
- 1 standard cup vanilla yogurt
- ½ cup standard sour cream
- 1 pint fresh blackberries
- ½ - 1 pint other berries, as garnish for topping (optional)

Directions:
Mix dairy ingredients in a big bowl. Add ½ amount (½ pint) of blackberries and blend in with mixed ingredients.
Fill the pie shell with blended ingredients. Utilize the remaining ½ pint of blackberries (and other berries, if desired) as decorative toppings to the pie. Chill in the fridge until ready to serve.

Daughter's Smoothie Superfood Breakfast
by
Michael (MJ) FitzGerald

Doctor Daughter Katie (Pediatrician & Anesthesiologist) tried to get Pops on the "straight and narrow" path to health with this recipe. Have to admit: it tastes great and you feel healthier for it!

Rev for the day!

Shopping List:

Fruits
bananas, frozen
blueberries, frozen
date

Veggies
cauliflower
kale

Powders
cocoa powder
plant-based protein powder (chocolate)

Seeds
flax
chia
hemp

Liquid
Almond milk

Here's Katie's smoothie recipe:

2 cups kale (fresh or frozen)
3-4 florets frozen cauliflower
1 cup frozen blueberries
½ cup (or ½ large) frozen banana
Small handful (less than ¼ cup) walnuts
1 tbsp ground flax seeds
1 tbsp chia seeds
1 tbsp hemp seeds
1 heaping tbsp cocoa powder (unsweetened)
1 scoop plant-based chocolate protein powder
1 date
1-2 tbsp real maple syrup (optional)
1 ½ cups almond milk
¾ cup water

Blend on high for several minutes to get it nice and smooth! It blends a bit easier if you leave all the ingredients sitting together in the blender for a few minutes first. I premake a week's worth in containers in the freezer, then in the morning, dump the contents in with the almond milk/water.

Makes one extra large or two smaller smoothies.

Packed full of nutrients, superfoods, healthy fats, and protein!!!

Recipe for Disaster (AKA Humble Pie)
by
Stefanie Hutcheson

1 First-Time Novelist	1 Published Book
1 Dining Experience	Favorite Husband
1 local bookstore	1 Waitress

Take the First-Time Novelist to a cafe of your choice. Add the Favorite Husband and discuss the Published Book. Sit that Novelist down where she can casually look around at the locals and smile at the ones who meet her eyes.

Discuss the accomplishment and how happy the Novelist is to have her book selling in this town. Add the waitress coming to your table at this time. Smile with humility as she says, "You must be Stefanie." Glow with pride at her recognition of Novelist's newfound fame. Graciously beam at her and agree that indeed, you are Stefanie. Engage with her and ask how she knows you. Try not to wither in your chair as she motions toward Favorite Husband and says, "I saw it on his shirt."

Politely place your order. Use the cool water supplied by the waitress to dip a napkin into as you try to wipe the embarrassment from your cheeks. Kick Favorite Husband discreetly under the table as he tries to hide his laughter at the dish of Humble Pie just served to you. Thank God that He only allows one serving of it.

Sausage Stars

From The Kitchen Of Stefanie Hutcheson

1 lb. cooked and crumbled sausage   1 lb. cooked and crumbled bacon
16 oz. sour cream   2 cups shredded cheddar cheese
3 Tbls. Ranch Dressing Mix (1 pkg)
50-100 wonton skins*, precooked in cupcake pans

Take the wonton skins and mold them into the cupcake pans. Bake at 350° until just gently browned, usually between 5-10 minutes. Meanwhile, mix the first five ingredients thoroughly. If you are short on time, you can use the pre-cooked bacon (I like to use the larger package, but the small one is fine too). Spoon the mixture into the wontons and rebake until the cheese is bubbly, usually 5-10 minutes more.

These are great hot or cold! You can place a small amount of the cooked mixture into an uncooked wonton wrapper, roll it into taquito shapes, and bake that way.

* Wonton skins--aka Egg Roll Wrappers--can be found in the grocery store's produce section.

Mississippi Roast
by
Stephen Downing

3 pounds or so chuck roast in a crockpot
Put the roast in the pot
Sprinkle with 1 Hidden Valley Ranch mix packet
Sprinkle with 1 McCormick Au Jus mix packet
1 stick of salted butter
5 pepperoncini peppers
Do not add water
Cook on low 7-8 hours

Flavor variations: add in onion soup mix, potatoes, and Philly cream cheese along with the other ingredients at the beginning.

Favorites

Making Sense Of It All
by
Stefanie Hutcheson

When the sun breaks through the clouds, illuminating them as though
they are outlined in brilliance;
When I top the hill and see Grandfather Mountain majestically sitting
in the distance;

When I hear the opening notes of a special song;
When I listen to the birds tweeting their praise;

When I walk into the theater and the popcorn is ready;
When the fire invites me with its crackling logs;

When the tea trickles down my throat, soothing and refreshing my
parched mouth;
When the first bite of ooey-gooey goodness hits my palette;

When welcoming arms tightly enfold me in their grasp;
When my fingers trace the words to an underlined script:

These are a few of my favorite things.

The Flight of Favorites
by
Kathy Lyday

After my mother died, I had a daylily named for her: Floye's Favorite. Fond of the early peach-colored bloomers, she would have been pleased at this choice, I believe. Others with whom I have shared these plants echo that sentiment. And when they bloom each summer, we all remember her.

A child chooses a favorite candy or a favorite toy and they move on from these to a favorite pet; a book they read in school to a most revered author. Then it is on to a favorite piece of clothing, a favorite place, a favorite food, a favorite team, song, movie, and then a favorite person. As life progresses, the favorites are often replaced.

What is the fate of the favorites? Imagine them boarding an airplane, all starting out in first class; some staying and others are moving back to coach over time. They remain old favorites–out of the limelight and in the shadows waiting to be brought forth for nostalgic reunion.

Favorites often move about. A coached favorite may find its way back to first class. Occasionally favorites are hijacked and end up leaving the plane. And it is possible for favorites to move up to the cockpit and take over completely. Something can become a favorite and then cease to be so—or a favorite can end up changing the course of a life.

A favorite holds its head high as long as it can serve a purpose. When life's journey ends, the plane lands, and the favorites are released, stardust swirling about the universe, seeking the opportunity to bestow favor upon others.

Go Take a Hike
by
Gretchen Griffith

Oval track morning
get those miles in my dear friend
boring necessity

Inside walk finished
nature beckons me outdoors
fresh beauty awaits

Broyhill Walking Park
geese and turtles on the pond
flowers to enjoy

An afternoon pause
name the trees, shoo the squirrels
River Walk strolling

Beacon Heights trail next
step over chunks of boulders
a view worth the trek

Aptly named Rough Ridge
up, over and up some more
no easy hike down

Totally renewed
filled with enthusiasm
favorites for walking

125

Exploring the Otherworld
by
Lucy Wilkes

Does life begin with a seed and a spark of light?

Rainwater and sunshine activate the life in the seed to produce tomatoes, squash, okra, and other yummy veggies.

Sneaking peeks to discover the first fruits from the earth. Under the umbrella of green, the leaves are bright yellow flowers with the promise of produce to eat.

Each morning the dew comes and gives the garden a drink: first the blade, then the plant, then the blossom, and then the prize. What a thrill to watch the yellow flower turn into a baby squash.

Discovering tiny white flowers peeking out from under the pale green leaves. A promise of beans that soon will be.

Down at the bottom of this garden jungle, what do I see? Yellow cucumber blossoms with a bee collecting pollen for honey.

However, the okra blossom is the loveliest of them all. On top of the plant, so tall, are pale white petals that form a cup with a crimson throat. Fried, steamed, sauteed, or grilled, then the flavor is to be savored.

For as the rain and the snow come down from heaven,
and do not return there without watering the earth,
and making it bear and sprout,
and furnishing seed to the sower and bread to the eater;
(Isaiah 55:10 The New American Standard)

A Duet of Favorites
by
Michael (MJ) FitzGerald

As a young man, devoid of sexual sophistication and nuance by virtue of a relatively innocent, insulated puberty, I sampled Melville and utterly rejected him in spasms of naive sarcasm. Clearly, I was a stranger to great literature.

Call me Paddy. A simple urban kid of asphalt playgrounds, vacant lots, alleys, rapid underground transit, stickball, Confiteors, and Latin classics. I knew nothing of whaling, nor did I care. My adolescent self-consciousness recoiled me from anything titled "Moby Dick." Such was the thin-shelled angst of city youth raised to think a kiss was a blessing, much less necking. Necking was the kick starter to all kinds of illicit, passionate things. This was not porn. It was an experimental exploration. Fantasized or realized behavior, however, did not extend in my mind to the suggestive literary imagery of the world.

Sure, city kids guffawed at the latest issue of *Playboy* or traded explicit citations of *Lady Chatterley's Lover* or St. Augustine's *Confessions* but the material of Sigmund Freud's introspection and analysis of the sexual subconscious was reserved for the more prescient and courageous among us. Not many of us were skilled in double entendres, or found comfort in the mere suspicion of sexual innuendo. Resultantly, Melville's title alone was enough to raise templates of murky sexual interpretation to this great sea-faring classic of a novel. This defense engendered - is this a permitted verb in this age of conditional pronouns? - caustic armaments at the reader mindset I had adopted to offset my natural, young reserve in tackling all literature smacking of symbolism.

I was merciless in my juvenile ridicule of chapters upon chapters of knots and cords, harpoons, and tattooed cultures. Then, when confronted with an entire chapter of drilling into a whale's head for buckets of sperm oil, to include a sailor's risk within such a confined space, I would not yield in harsh critique until I had classmates smothering their laughter by means of a simple eye roll beneath the teacher's nose. I learned precious little of the exquisite

Melville that year, but came away with fond memories of youthful mischief.

Then, upon returning to him as an adult, I read, with better perspective, not only the enthralling tale *Moby Dick* is, but also the immersive, near-mystical prose of this consummate artist, Herman Melville. I offer, by way of illustration, only one of literally scores of passages crafted to convey the pure artistic expression, through honed characters, of man's existence, his limited agency with the sea and Nature, and his consequent insights.

Here is a favorite:

> *"...rainbows do not visit the clear air; they only irradiate vapour. And so, through all the thick mist of the dim doubts of my mind, divine intuitions now and then shoot, enkindling my fog with a heavenly ray. And for this I thank God; for all have doubts; many deny; but doubts or denials, few along with them, have intuitions. Doubts of all things earthly, and intentions of some things heavenly;*
> *This combination makes neither believer nor infidel, but makes a man who regards them both with equal eye."* Melville (verbatim)

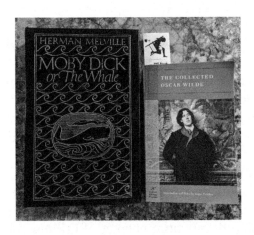

The case for a favorite European author is straightforward enough. Oscar Wilde, the winsome Irish playwright, poet, prose, and essay author showcases both the shallow and profound in literature with characteristic wit, elegant "versatility, and incisive critique." Wilde consistently excelled whenever he poised his pen. Interior decor in America as portrayed in art, the flaws of the English Renaissance, London's well-lit stage, Europe's grim novels, and the lack of lying (vs. realism) in art. All provided a backdrop to his wit and wisdom, despite Wilde's tragic marriage, public scandal, and imprisonment. Oxford-educated, he had the skill set and resolution to contend with his adversities.

Here are some favorite samples of Wilde's witty touchés and insights:

*Only the shallow know themselves.
*The old believe everything: the middle-aged suspect everything: the young know everything.
*The well-bred contradict other people. The wise contradict themselves.
*To love oneself is the beginning of a life-long romance.
*The amount of women in London who flirt with their own husbands is perfectly scandalous. It looks so bad. It is simply washing one's clean linen in public.
*It is awfully hard work doing nothing. However, I don't mind hard work where there is no definite object of any kin.
*In literature, we require distinction, charm, beauty, and imaginative power.
*...the basis of life - the energy of life, as Aristotle would call it - is simply the desire for expression, and Art is always presenting various forms through which this expression can be attained.
*...the difference between unimaginative realism and imaginative reality.

Promptly Speaking

Each of our weekly Foothills Writers meetings has time for us to respond to a writing prompt. The timer is set for six minutes and--barring technology complications--we feverishly scratch our heads and hope to come up with some priceless jewel that will do the prompt justice.

Most of the time, we have no prior knowledge of the prompt. But for one of our assignments, we were given a little preliminary advance on the topic. We were to pen our thoughts about why **Billy Joe MacAllister jumped off the Tallahatchie Bridge** or to discuss what was thrown off of it. What you will read next is what we came up with. Following that, you will get to read about another response we had to a different prompt of our choosing as we share with you what we thought was some of our best.

Six minutes are sometimes just not enough to delve into what we are inspired by. However, that's what we do and we are almost always impressed with the results. We hope you will be too!

Ode to Billy Joe: What Did They Throw Off The Tallahatchie Bridge?

Stephen Downing

Billy Joe and Bobbi were secret lovers. Bobbi was pregnant...

Before Bobbi began showing she went into labor and gave birth to a stillborn premature baby girl. She and Billy Joe were terrified and at their wits' end as to what to do.

They wrapped their daughter in a blanket and rather than bury her, tossed her into the river, weighted down with a couple of rocks.

Billy Joe immediately felt remorse for their behavior. He later went back to the bridge to contemplate what he and Bobbi had done. Filled with shame, guilt, and a deep loathing of his actions, he jumped into the dark waters below...

Michael FitzGerald

Billie Joe McCallister jumped off the Tallahatchie bridge because he believed his preacher a bit too much. Ol' Rev. Sampson Thatcher was not only an old-time preacher, he was an Old Testament haranguer of the vengeful, jealous God of early Israel and its prophets. Other sinful cities and states merited destruction across the board. The sinful in David's kingdom, the kingdom of the Jews - especially those who did not heed the prophets- also merited divine vengeance.

Billie Joe was convinced he was a sinner of the first order ever since he and she lay in the woods and explored each other, giving in to their mutual lengthy and youthful romance. Then it ended. And then Preacher Thatcher's continual proscription to read and realize the reality of Psalm 88 was linked in Billie Joe's sorrow to the ol' testament "word" as he understood it. "My only friend is darkness" and so are the depths of the Tallahatchie.

Stefanie Hutcheson

"So, Billie Joe, why did you jump? I mean, seriously dude, is anything worth losing your life over?"

"Do you know me?" He nearly sneered.

"Um, no, sir. Only what I've heard sung about you. Gulp. Embarrassed pause. Would you like to tell me your side of things? Just for the record. You don't have to if you don't want to."

He studied me for a moment, drew a heavy sigh, and seemed to wrestle within himself. Finally, he spoke.

"All right. But please, hold your comments, judgments, and so on until I finish. Agreed?"

I nodded.

"Bobbie and I were friends. Not boyfriend/girlfriend but just...friends. We'd grown up together and knew each other sometimes better than ourselves. She could tell me anything, as I could her, but you don't really need to know that just now.

"Bobbie had been...taken advantage of, shall we say? We used to meet up here on the bridge each Wednesday. She told me something, someone, had been..."

He paused. Looking up to the sky, he seemed to be searching for the right words. After a moment he continued.

Looking deeply into my eyes, making sure there wasn't any criticism there, he went on.

"It was her uncle. Saul." He nearly spat the name out. "He'd been doing things ain't proper for any man to do to a gal, 'specially one he's kin to. The first time, Bobbie was shocked. Confused. And angry. Her momma never told her what men could turn into with a little whiskey in 'em.

"And see? He'd been...

"Look, let's cut to the chase. I killed him. I had to. I couldn't let Bobbie keep being hurt like that. He looked pleadingly at me, seeking understanding, seeking...forgiveness? I only meant to scare him but I guess I hit 'im too hard. Anyways, I had to make it look like an accident. She and I threw the shovel off the bridge but when I went back to clean up the mess, I couldn't take it. Couldn't take the fact that I had taken a man's life.

"Eye for an eye, right? I took his. 'Twas only right I had to give up mine too."

He paused. I nodded at him, hearing what he hadn't said. I reached my hand out to him, to show Billie he'd done the right thing. "Your secret is safe with me."

He smiled, looked at the muddy waters, and was gone. Again. I took my flowers, tossed them into the Tallahatchie, and made my way home.

Kathy Lyday

Billie Jo McAllister jumped off the Tallahatchie Bridge because he was searching for the money that he had thrown off the bridge earlier with his girlfriend, Bobbie. He had stolen the offering money that had been collected at church the Sunday night before. He and Bobbie wanted to run off together and have a nest egg as a startup. It was his luck that little Katy and Keith Kelly had chosen this particular evening to empty their piggy banks, and they had been saving awhile. There were several pounds of coins and Billie Joe and Bobbie wrapped them up in a watertight package, certain that they would sink to the bottom due to the weight. Billie Joe had made it all the way through the sixth grade.

Billie Joe later jumped off to retrieve the package because he was afraid of the snakes that were on the river bank. Unfortunately for Billie Joe, his trajectory was off and he hit his head on a rock and floated down river. Billie Joe's body washed up on the bank. Brother Taylor did not preach the funeral; he had moved to another church by then. Talk was that offering money had been a little short from time to time.

Some months later, the brother and Becky Thompson were fishing on the river bank. They weren't worried about the snakes. Becky hooked something and the brother had to help her pull it up. Turned out to be the coins that Billie Joe had thrown off the bridge. They got to looking at the coins and found some rare buffalo nickels that had imperfections.

How do you think they got the money to buy that store in Tupelo?

Gretchen Griffith

It's been a year. It's been a hundred flowers. At least. Nothing works. No flowers dropped into the dark depths have eased my pain.

He eased his pain the only way he could. He chose the easy way out. Who was the real coward, him or me, the one who should have held his hand and jumped alongside him? I'm the one who faces reality

134

day after day. The one who stares at the back of his mother's head in the pew, not in her eyes, mind you, but in the increasing grayness of the back of her bowed head deep in prayer on Sunday mornings.

We were on top of the world, the two of us. We had a future. But we had a baby that no one knew about, delivered by him in the woodshed after hiding it in my expanding blouse for months. I heard its cry. He heard my screams, not only from the pain of childbirth, but also from the tremendous agony that our worst wishes had come true.

We wrapped it in cloth, swaddling clothes, except that we didn't put it in a manger. We threw it off the Tallahatchie Bridge.

The same bridge I stand on today and pray for my redemption from the guilt.

Thomas Blanton

As they were courting, Billy Joe and the girl were spending time together picking flowers on Choctaw Ridge and tossing them into the river below the bridge as they talked about their dreams for a future together.

The preacher that the mother was hoping would woo and marry her daughter was out riding around and saw the young couple, but the fact of this being courtship didn't register on the girl's mother.

Because of the father's strong opposition, Billy Joe couldn't have the girl. Her father ran him off every time he would come around. Apparently, he didn't have enough money or backbone to elope with her, so he committed suicide as the only way out he could imagine.

Within the year, the father was dead and the older brother was married and had moved away, so there would have been nothing standing in the way of Billy Joe getting the girl he loved and living a life of wedded bliss with her.

So now, every day, she grieves by reenacting their courtship ritual with the flowers at the bridge, watching them float away the way her dreams had.

Lucy Wilkes

This is the saddest song I've heard. The music is great. The poetic words are enjoyable. However, the reason Billy Joe

jumped from the bridge is a mystery. His heart and soul must have been distraught beyond what he could bear. The girl still remembers him each spring when the flowers bloom. Each person deals with grief in different ways. The event is saved through music for all to share and wonder about. The only ones who really know are the ones who were there.

Random Prompts

Linda McLaughlin LaRose
Prompt: spend one million dollars in one hour.

My mission, to spend one million dollars and I only have an hour before the cartel discovers I am in their Cayman Islands bank account. Alexa, call the senator. Sir—How fast can you get me out to the reservation? I have the money. Before tomorrow we will be home free, all the Dine will have running water, wifi, and a start to getting more clinics into the less traveled areas. Meet me at the helicopter pad. Cover me, I'm going in. And Senator, I still have those pictures from Jeffrey. Make it snappy.

Lucy Wilkes
Prompt title: Women who inspire.

In my life there are a lot of women who inspired me. First and foremost is my mom. She is the one who adopted me and took me as her own child. Second is my grandma, who taught me about the Lord and how to pray.

In the tenth grade, I had an English teacher who encouraged me to be what I could be. The class assignment was to write about all authors we studied in English literature. This task seemed too large for me so she gave me one story to write on. I made an A on the assignment because she made it smaller for me to handle.

Michael (MJ) FitzGerald
Prompt: A Lesson I Am Still Learning

A lesson I am still learning is the one where that special person may not be the lifelong or even the long-term partner you assumed when romance blossomed. The fortunate, dutiful, or determined are often blessed with an intimate relationship, but it is no longer a given, or even the odds on favorite, it once was.

Much of our parents' generation assumed it was a lifelong irrevocable commitment, and lived it. Our generation (post-WWII) discovered differently. My bride and I came from families with celebrated 50-year anniversaries.

Our children do not have such illusions and know there is plain ol' chance, along with discerning skills of relationships involved. Without consistent, default affection, however, does chance or skills matter?

Steve Downing
Prompt: A Pet Peeve

Socks! Escaping from the laundry - leaping to the side while I try to stuff them into the washer.

After being successfully cleaned, escaping from the washer onto the laundry floor while in transit to the dryer. (Sometimes hiding by sticking high up to the washer tub wall.)

After being dried, they will again slip out onto the floor while being moved to the living room couch for folding. Often, a lone sock will seek refuge by hiding in a fitted bed sheet's corner.

All my athletic socks are identical. I don't know if they are supposed to be monogamous, but I'm willing to bet that over time they rarely routinely 'hook-up' with the same partner.

Mission accomplished when I finally get them all off the floor and into the sock drawer!

Carol Starr
Prompt: You get up Christmas morning and see a sleigh overturned in your backyard and hear noises coming from your chimney.

Next thing I knew here comes some chimney ash, all over our nice clean carpet. The dog started to bark. "Hush!" I said, "or you won't get a squeaky toy."

"Santa, why are you late?"

"It must have been the scotch whiskey and shortbread I ate at the Ross's house. My, that shortbread was good. But it weighed me down. The reindeer could hardly get the sleigh off the roof. Not to mention I was disoriented. From now on, I'll stick to milk and cookies."

He went straight to his work. and missed all the stockings, the plastered old jerk, and laying his fingers aside of his nose, straight up the chimney he rose. The chimney was pretty clean after that. The children got their toys and the dog got his squeaky toy.

Kathy Lyday
Prompt: Pet Peeves

Whether in the grocery store or on a walk with your dog, using plastic bags on a roll is such a convenience–if you can get them open. You don't have to remember to bring a basket or a mesh bag for your produce to the store; you can stand there trying to open your bag while watching your avocados ripen. By the time you get to the cashier, she can see the number on that sticker through the bag and that will help her, because she doesn't know what avocados are. It will help you see the number, as well as save time when you go through self-checkout, because you are purchasing dragonfruit.

Bags for dogs that fit into the little cylinder attached to your dog's leash allow you to keep the dog-walking area pristine. You can be standing out in the cold trying to separate one of those bags and ready to scoop when a mother drives past to drop off her child at school. You can use the still unopened bag to wave at her as she drives back by. This is particularly the case in cold weather. The best way to circumvent this is to separate your bags at home and put them in your pockets. That way you don't have to spend extra time out in the cold looking like a crazy person.

Stefanie Hutcheson
Prompt: Recall a plea your teenage self made to your parents.

"Momma, please, please, please get us out of here. You know how mean he is."

Momma glanced sympathetically at me, and maybe she even brushed my shoulder. She looked around to make sure he hadn't somehow come in and was eavesdropping on our conversation. In a hushed tone she told me, "I'm sorry that he hits you. You know the beer makes him act mean."

I could see where this was--wasn't going. The excuses for Dad's behavior were numerous. If it wasn't the beer, it was the Navy. If it

138

wasn't the Navy, it was being back in North Carolina and him not having a job. If it wasn't him not having a job, it was because he didn't really know how to love. If it wasn't because he didn't really know how to love, it was because he wouldn't go to church with us. If it wasn't because he wouldn't go to church with us, it must somehow be my fault.

"Try to stay on his good side. Don't argue with him."

"But, Momma…" I started to protest.

"Shhh. I think I hear him coming. Tell you what: if he ever hits Billy, then we'll leave. Sound good?"

In brokenness I hung my head, wiped my tears, and prayed so hard. Prayed that I would be good and yet a part of me prayed he'd hit Billy. Just once. To see if Momma would finally know how to love.

Thomas Blanton
Prompt: Fractured Fairy Tales

The call came in at 11:24. Break-in at Mama Bear's place. Sheesh! What's with all this Bed and Breakfast stuff? Seems everybody is getting into the Air BnB trend.

They reported a prowler in their house. Uninvited guest?

Questioned Papa Bear: New guests were to arrive this afternoon. After breakfast for the family, they had to run errands to get ready for guests. While the family was out, a prowler broke in and raided the pantry, spilling food, leaving the refrigerator open, and eggs and milk spilled on the floor.

Questioned Mama Bear: When they arrived and saw the damage in the kitchen they went through the rest of the house and found sofa cushions on the floor, chairs overturned, one antique chair broken.

Questioned Bear, Jr.: They checked the bedrooms and found all of the beds unmade, dirt in the beds, and a blonde woman sleeping in the bed they had prepared for today's guests.

I asked the father about this and he confirmed his wife and son's account. He added that when they woke the woman, she escaped by jumping out the window and they immediately called 911.

The forensics team investigated the perimeter and found evidence of a hard fall below a second-floor window. We checked with all the local hospitals and found the suspect had gone in with a broken leg and was still in treatment.

The Bear family identified her in a lineup. Her trial begins in two weeks.

Gretchen Griffith
Prompt: Describe your favorite pet.

I've said some famous last words in my time here on earth, like the time our cat Sam died and I said "That's it. No more pets. We're through."

We'd been through cats and dogs and goldfish and gerbils and an outdoor lizard that my son claimed I couldn't kill. But now the children have grown and moved on and my husband and I were done with all things pet related, especially since the favorite thing of college-age kiddos seemed to be to pay a fortune for cute pets in the windows and bring them home for mama to keep until they graduated and got their own place. Sure.

So we were a pet-free couple until some unkind soul dumped a kitten in our driveway.

Nine years later, this now grown kitten is sound asleep on the pillow of my long ago moved away daughter's bed, perfectly happy in her home.

When she kicks the bucket, I'm serious. No more pets.

Author Bios

Thomas Blanton

Thomas Blanton is named for his father, Thomas Edmund, Sr. "Thomas" means "twin," and his father was, indeed, a twin. He is a native of North Carolina's foothills. He and his wife have eight grandchildren between them.

Thomas is a United Methodist minister, a former media producer for Fayetteville Technical Community College, an appliance salesman for Sears and Home Depot, and an adjunct professor of Religion for Gardner-Webb University.

He is the author of *The Unintentional Gospel: The Gospel According to Jesus' Enemies*. Under the pen name of Thomas Ballantine, he is the author of *Ridge Runner* and the upcoming novel, *Who Killed Me?* currently being serialized on Amazon's Kindle Vella.

Stephen Downing

Steve is a retired Marine Corps pilot, a retired high school science teacher, and now a wannabe writer. He is part Peter Pan and part curmudgeon. Perpetually lazy, Steve is prone to procrastination. He is slowly working to finish and publish a collection of short stories to be entitled *Not Fairytales*. (Maybe this year?)

Steve is father to three lovely ladies and Paw Paw to five grandkids.

Originally from the West Coast, he is married to Carolyn, who is a Rhodhiss native. He enjoys life in the foothills of western North Carolina.

He is especially indebted to the Foothills Writers Group for their help, love, and support. Thought I'd butter 'em up.

Michael (MJ) FitzGerald

I am a veteran father who has degrees in English literature, sociology, and business. I was blessed with loving parents and, as a result, started out with, basically, a positive self-image. My parents were devout Roman Catholics - my mother all her life, every day of it. My dad nearly every day of it!

Catholicism in the mid-twentieth century placed considerable emphasis on "saying the rosary." The Holy Rosary is the silent or aloud recitation of the beaded, rhythmic, and repetitive prayers to Mary, the Mother of God. The purpose of this devotional prayer is to seek Mary's intercession with her Son, Jesus, on our behalf.

An important, unique element of the rosary is the Prayer to St. Michael the Archangel, seeking "...protection against the wickedness and snares of the Devil..." I guess everyone likes to think there is a big league angel looking out for them, in addition to their Guardian Angel. For this reason, I suspect, my parents and Catholics in general had a certain fondness for the name "Michael."

I know I took a distinct pride in being Michael whenever we prayed the rosary. It was pretty cool to be named after the guy who drove Lucifer and his crew out of heaven.

Gretchen Griffith

Gretchen Griffith enjoys catching stories and turning them into books. How she got her name is one of her favorite catches. During World War II, her father worked in the boatyards building ships, one of which wasn't ready until after the final battles had been fought and the

ink dried on the treaties. Her father and very pregnant mother attended the launching ceremony. The admiral's wife had the honor of christening it. When she broke the wine bottle over the ship's bow, she announced in a clear voice, "I christen thee..." whatever. Gretchen's mother didn't remember the name when she told the story years later. What she did remember was the name of the admiral's wife, Gretchen. She turned to her husband and said, "If this baby is a girl, let's name her Gretchen," and the rest is history.

Stefanie Hutcheson

Ahh, who doesn't have one, two, or thirteen names by which s/he is called or referred to--both in and out of public hearing? In my lifetime, I have had a few.

Most recently, my nickname is Grandolph, courtesy of my lovely three grandsons. They came up with this--in part--due to the Tolkein quote on my car about wandering. It is often interspersed with Oldilocks.

My favorite SIL often calls me Granny Snef. This is because many years ago before he was a part of our family Steve's cousins were down from Michigan. Sabrina, who was probably around seven at the time, lisped a little, and instead of calling me Stef slipped and called me Snef. Yeah, that one lives on in infamy.

My hubby pretty much calls me Stef or Granny--except when we get into our roles of silliness. Then I am Mabel to his George, Jenni to his Forrest, or old woman when he thinks I am supposed to be in the kitchen.

As a child, my nickname was Skipper. My Uncle Steve called me that because I liked to go fishing with him and my dad. My sister Mary called me Stink Stink the Devil or Stef-fanny after years of me calling her Moo Moo The Cow. She thought this to be hilarious.

My writers' groups have a few choice names for me as well. Whippersnapper, Grammar Nazi, or Missy. These are the ones they call me to my face. Behind it though? Hmn. I'm not sure I want to know.

Linda McLaughlin LaRose

Linda McLaughlin LaRose was indulged as a child in her writing fantasy by her grandmother and teachers who submitted her poetry and allowed her to produce her plays on stage. An English

professor submitted one of her stories to a contest judged by a Pulitzer Prize-winning novelist and she won first place, giving Linda permission to come out of the closet and write "for real." Her first novel burned up in a house

144

fire and she mourned her characters like they had died there in those ashes. Linda is continuing to play like she is a writer with the Foothill Writers Group while she works on her novel-in-progress, *Ida Claire Beaucatcher*, who is fed up and ready to talk.

Kathy Lyday

Kathy Lyday is a former Media Coordinator, who retired from the Caldwell County Schools System. Dividing her time between Wilmington and Hickory, she is blessed to have two married daughters and a grandson. Kathy enjoys working with dogs and she and her therapy dog, Russell, visit various spots around Hickory.

Recently, a writer friend reminded Kathy of a quote by Anne Lamott: "You own everything that happened to you. Tell your stories. If people wanted you to write warmly about them, they should have behaved better." Her keyboard has not been idle since!

Kathy is humbled to have been accepted into the Foothills Writers Group this year and is eternally grateful for their encouragement.

Carol Starr

Carol is a Canadian Northerner. She spent grade-school years where summer nights were light all night and winter nights were dark from 4:00 pm to 10:00 am. The small things of nature bloomed frantically during the short summers. In the winter, Northern Lights waved green curtains in a cold, starry sky.

Later, in eastern Canada's British Columbia province, she lived in one of six mining company houses on a mountainside in the Cascade Mountains, then in a smelter city on the cold, swift-moving and mighty Columbia River.

Finally, Carol moved to New Jersey, and finished high school in a commuter town near New York City, learning about Villager clothes and other preppy things (such as how to eat pizza) from up-scale classmates. There was even a school cafeteria, so, no more lunchboxes.

College was in Iowa, where she earned a BFA in pottery. Carol began work as a draftsman and later as a Museum Village potter for three summers in the New York Hudson valley.

After the death of her first husband, she went back to school, graduated from Columbia University with a Master of Architecture, and became an architect. During that time, she remarried.

She retired to North Carolina where she lives contentedly with her husband, Elliott, and their large, rambunctious dog, Casper.

Carol likes to write Haiku poems because they are short and deal with the natural world. In Haiku, every word counts.

Carol is also writing (slowly) about her father's life and her family's many adventures.

Lucy Wilkes

Let's think about a name.

Where does the name come from? Family, friends, someone famous, or did it come in a dream?

This author was named by her birth mother. Her adoptive mother and father kept it. She was named after her biological mother's younger sister whose name was Lucille June.

So life began for this little one. She was wanted by her adoptive parents, grandparents, and family. She grew up being loved and a bit spoiled. Two years and nine months later her parents had a baby boy of their own.

Growing up with a baby brother was an adventure for Lucille June. She always had a companion to play with. However, as the two grew into maturity, the older took the role of firstborn, sassy, demanding, and bossy. This attitude did not sit well with her younger brother. He would not play when she wanted him to, so she would pick on him until he chased her. Lucille June was delighted he was playing whether he realized it or not. This became her favorite pastime.

Lucille June changed high schools in the tenth grade and her name became Lucy June as she was called by her new classmates. The name stuck. After graduation, Lucy chose to go to Florida Beauty College in Jacksonville, Florida.

The Cosmetology profession became her passion. The artist's gifts became an expression of the medium called hair. She made a living in Cosmetology and had fun doing it. Who could ask for anything more?

Lucy married the love of her life in October 1982. As a couple, they taught Sunday School, Private Home School, and traveled on mission trips to Chile, South America. Lucy taught Bible, Journalism, and Physics at the school. The Journalism class even published a yearbook.

In the fall of 1994, a move was made to North Carolina to be part of a small church in Morganton that still is thriving.

Lucy became a cosmetology instructor at Caldwell Community College and Technical Institute, where she taught for five years.

Lucy has one daughter, three grandsons, and one great-grandson. She wrote her first story as a challenge to her grandson to bring him up to his fifth reading grade level. And he did. Lucy wrote a story and made him a superhero in it. Thus, *Cackle Packle and Friends* became her first published book.

Lucy thought and thought. What about a novel for her older grandson? Could she really do that? She joined an author's group that encouraged her to write the next book. *Trev Tracker* was published after three years of writing adventures. After retiring and joining the Foothills Writers and Quirky Quillers, she is working on her third book with the groups.

Lucy lives happily ever after in Hudson, North Carolina.

148

From our first Writers Weekend Retreat at the Outer Banks, NC

Made in the USA
Monee, IL
01 October 2022

15023597R00089